Teach Your
3-7 Year Old Math

By John Bowman

Teach Your 3-7 Year Old Math

© 2014 John Bowman

ISBN #: 9780989176859

Published By: Montessori At Home!
Bradenton, FL
jbowmanbooks@gmail.com

Cover Photos: *Top right: Montessori Print Shop, bottom left: Shutterstock*

The information presented here is for parents to use as they see fit, according to their time, interest, and capabilities. Not all parents will see the same results using the activities shown here. No guarantees are made or implied. Success with early learning activities requires the right approach to encourage a child's interest and enthusiasm, and consistency over time. Math skills develop in a sequence, and following it will give the best results. The author receives no compensation or other benefits from any of the providers of materials, apps, or other resources recommended in this book. All are suggested on the basis of their quality and value for parents working with their children at home.

All adults working with young children should **keep safety in mind first**. Children under three should not use small objects that could cause choking without continuous supervision. Look out for sharp points and edges and be sure your child handles learning materials carefully.

Table of Contents

Introduction

My life's most enjoyable, rewarding work was being a Montessori Primary (3-6 year olds) Teacher and Director. Preschool age children, IMO, are the coolest people on the planet.

This eBook focuses on teaching 3-7 year olds about mathematics and geometry using the Montessori math sequence for preschoolers, modified to make it easy and inexpensive to teach your 3-7 year old at home. This approach to helping children master math skills has been working beautifully for over one hundred years. You can use the same process at home.

Helping children learn about math is fun. Math is logical sequential, and has different aspects for variety. As your child masters each step you move into the Decimal System, operations with numbers, fractions, geometry, and practical math applications. Teachers get to enjoy seeing young children develop new math skills. I hope more parents can have the same experiences right at home.

There is no need for children to grow up disliking math! Using the activities shown here with your 3 – 6 year old for a year or two, she will be doing math at a 2nd - 3rd grade level, with no pressure or stress. Just as important, he will develop a positive, confident attitude about math, built on successful experiences with these activities.

These activities can also help 6-7 year old children who are struggling with math. Starting at the beginning and progressing through the sequence of activities shown here can fill in gaps in a child's math understanding and set things on a successful path.

Early success in the school environment is the best way to insure future success. Children who start strong progress more easily. They believe in themselves and their abilities, and come to see themselves as people who are successful with math and other work. Since our limitations are largely in our own minds, this is half the battle won.

Have fun with your child. Be patient, positive, and encouraging. Allow your child time to practice and truly master each step. Expand what your child learns about numbers into your daily life activities. If you do this, you will have wonderful experiences watching your child develop solid math skills. I encourage you to expand your home early learning activities into other areas, such as Practical Life, Sensorial, Science, and Language.

Early learning activities help children develop strong brain architecture, a positive and confident self-image, a love of learning, and practical abilities that prepare them for going out into the world. I hope many more parents have the wonderful experience of helping their children develop these positive personality characteristics and life skills.

John Bowman

Also by the author:

Montessori At Home!

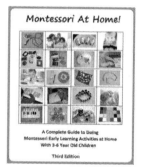

www.montessoriathomebook.com

The Third Edition is a 576 page, $10.95 pdf eBook guide to doing an entire Montessori preschool program at home. Complete Montessori how-to information for parents, over 300 activities in Practical Life, Sensorial, Art & Music, Digital Life, Science, Mathematics, Writing, and Reading, hundreds of links to sites, blogs, and videos to expand on the information in the eBook, an extensive collection of printables, and recommendations for over 200 of the very best educational digital tablet apps. The best value in early childhood education for parents.

Download Your Math Printables

To download a free set of printable materials for use with many of the activities, visit this URL:

http://www.montessoriathomebook.com/Home.html/math-printables/

Click the link provided there to download a pdf file with your printables. Save a copy to a flash drive so you won't lose it if your computer crashes. I recommend 67 lb. card stock or 110 lb. index for added durability. The copy centers at office supply stores and most crafts stores have these in colors by the sheet. Astrobright or other brightly colored papers can add interest to your materials. Most office supply stores have cold laminating sheets that allow you to laminate favorite materials for added durability without a heat laminating machine.

Materials for making geometric shapes

If you want to make extra - durable materials you can use science project display board or 14 point illustration board, available at most office supply stores. A pair of shears makes these easy to cut. You can print out the printables on paper, cut them out, and use paper spray glue to attach them securely to the stronger base materials to make them more durable.

Printables online

Search online when you need a specific printable and you will almost always find numerous good options. Here are a few excellent online suppliers of inexpensive and free printable materials that are perfect for parents working with their children at home:

Montessori Print Shop

Montessori for Everyone

Montessori Mom

Montessori Materials

Enchanted Learning

First School

Education.com

Kidsparkz.com

Kidslearningstation.com

preschoolpalace.org

k5learning.com

kidzone.ws

Making your own printable materials

Many math materials can be made on the fly using index cards, post-it notes, regular paper, a marker, and scissors. Things like + and = signs and numeral cards are easy to make quickly. Sometimes it is better to do this and capture a moment of spontaneous interest rather than wait to print something out on the computer and find your child has moved on to other things.

Store your printables in envelopes or zip lock bags and keep them with your child's math materials so they are always ready for use. If they become worn, torn, or bent, print out or make new ones.

Helping Young Children Learn

The early years are when the majority of our brain architecture is formed for life. Until around age 6, a child's brain is fluid, rapidly evolving, and wide open for input. Children open as many as *700 new brain nerve pathways every second* during the years from birth to six. This is when we can best help a child develop a stronger, more capable brain for life.

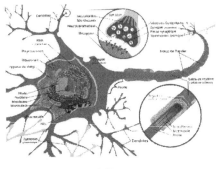

A Nerve

From birth to around six, children have what Maria Montessori called 'Absorbent Minds'. Early childhood is a unique time of rapid learning and brain development. As the folks at the Center on the Developing Child at Harvard University (developingchild.harvard.edu) put it:

"Early experience has a unique advantage in shaping the architecture of developing brain circuits before they are fully mature and stabilized."

"The quality of a child's early environment and the availability of appropriate experiences at the right stages of development are crucial in determining the strength or weakness of the brain's architecture."

"The exceptionally strong influence of early experiences on brain architecture makes the early years of life a period of both great opportunity and great vulnerability for brain development."

"Early learning lays the foundation for later learning, and is essential for the development of optimized brain architecture."

Young children typically experience natural Sensitive Periods to learning about numbers and language sometime in their late third or fourth year, continuing until they are five or six. Skills are more easily absorbed during these sensitive periods than at any other time of life. If we take advantage of these naturally occurring periods of heightened interest and ability, children's brain architecture, understanding, and life skills develop in an optimal way.

From the Center on the Developing Child:

"...specific experiences affect specific brain circuits during specific developmental stages – referred to as sensitive periods – it is vitally important to take advantage of these early opportunities in the developmental building process."

Or, as Maria Montessori stated:

"When one of these psychic passions is exhausted, another is enkindled. Childhood thus passes from conquest to conquest in a constant rhythm that constitutes its joy and happiness."

Early learning activities do much more than teach math, writing, and reading. They help a child develop a positive, confident self-image and a true love of learning. This is the perfect preparation for success and fulfillment in school and life. The early years are always the time to start.

Young children require varying amounts of time and practice to master skills. A child who has the great fortune to be introduced to numbers in the early years, when he is most receptive to it by nature, acquires a marvelous foundation for all later math work. Success breeds success in skills development. A child who enters school already reading and doing basic math will experience quick success with schoolwork, setting the stage for continued success right through her entire education.

You do not need a teaching degree to help your 3-6 year old learn about numbers, fractions, and geometry. All it takes is your time, patience, encouragement, and following the sequence of activities in this book. Math lends itself perfectly to a logical sequence of activities you can easily provide while you track your child's progress. Your child will learn about numbers in a natural, stress-free way; and acquire a positive attitude toward number work.

You will have the great satisfaction of having made a positive difference in his development and future. Nice for you both!

Young children are processing and organizing millions of sensory inputs and exploring the world through movement. As Maria Montessori observed:

"Watching a child makes it obvious that the development of his mind comes through his movements. Since it is through movement that the will realizes itself, we should assist a child in his attempts to put his will into act."

Montessori especially noted that children 'take possession of the world with their hands':

"The hands are the instruments of man's intelligence. The human hand allows the mind to reveal itself."

All of this means that young children learn best by handling three dimensional objects and interacting directly with the real world, rather than virtual-digital or fantasy worlds. Helping young children learn is best done with materials that use real objects in interesting ways. Montessori created an enormous variety of such materials, which are found in Montessori preschools all over the world.

This book recommends a selection of original Montessori and other good learning materials to help your child master math skills and concepts. Most of the activities in this book use common, inexpensive items. You will not need to spend hours or a lot of money creating complicated, expensive materials.

The cost of the few Montessori and commercial materials recommended here is about $200. If your child uses them over a two year period, that's under $20/month to give your child a foundation of math knowledge for a lifetime – not bad. These materials last through use by multiple children, so you can sell them later and recover half or more of their cost. You could also share their cost with other parents of preschoolers and rotate them between homes.

If you can divert just a portion of what you would otherwise spend on disposable plastic toys over 1-3 years to obtaining the affordable, high quality learning materials recommended here, your budget will never notice it and your child's development will really benefit.

The important thing is to present all learning materials as special items. Then you give your child plenty of opportunities to practice in a positive atmosphere of encouragement and discovery. This is how strong brain architecture and a love of learning are developed in young children.

You will also find recommendations for good iPad and android apps throughout this book. Young children need most of their experiences to come from handling real objects, using all their senses, exploring the real world, and interacting with other people. Another vital developmental task of the years from 3-6, however, is acquiring the capacity for abstract thought.

In the first years of life, children use all their senses to gather an incredible storehouse of information about the real world. Once enough of these experiences are on board in a child's brain, she starts to think about the world mentally, like older children and adults. By the time a child is ready to learn about abstract symbols like letters and numerals, she is also ready to start using tablet apps.

No worries, schedules, or lesson plans

Early learning should be a joyous process of exploration, discovery, and fun. Pressure and stress have no place in these activities. As parents, we naturally want our children to shine. Since children imitate us, we can see them as reflections of ourselves, and may be anxious if they do not learn quickly. We may compare them to other children. You may have these feelings, but they need to be left out of your learning activities at home.

The title of this chapter purposely does not use the word teaching. Instead, we are *helping* children learn. Early learning is not a formal process where the student is an empty vessel to be filled with the teacher's wisdom. Young children have all the motivational drive they need, and the ability to adapt to the world, already within them. We are simply helping to optimize a natural process of growth and development that has unfolded within all children throughout history, even if adults do not help them that much.

Each child has an inner guide directing her development. The energy and motivation for learning come from within the child rather than being imposed from without by a schedule, lesson plan, or gold stars as a reward. Young children have a strong natural curiosity about the world and tons of energy. It is important to see your home activities as *supporting and helping* your child's inner guide, rather than directing the process.

Instead of creating lesson plans schedules, and other outer structure, it is more effective to create an activity and experience rich environment and encourage your child to use it. You allow and encourage repetition of favorite activities until your child achieves real mastery.

Your child has her own developmental pace. Going with the flow is the best practice. Let your child's spontaneous interests on a daily basis be your guide. Children are naturally drawn to the experiences they need in order to develop properly. When working with your preschool age child, keep these points in mind:

Be patient

Patience is a necessity when working with preschoolers. Little children have a natural plan for their development unfolding from within them. Montessori called it the 'Inner Teacher'. We often superimpose our ideas about how, what, and when children should learn by using lesson plans and weekly schedules. This is what happened for many of us in school, so we can unwittingly repeat the process with our children. This is not only unnecessary, it holds children back. They learn much more effectively when we follow the child and encourage their natural process of development by creating an activity-rich environment that supports it.

This is what happens in Montessori and other good preschools. The result is children who, by six, are reading well and doing math at what is considered an advanced level, all without a hint of pressure or stress, in an environment full of the joy of discovery and exploration.

Your child's spontaneously expressed interests are always your best guide as to what materials and activities to provide. See what attracts and holds your child's attention, and do more of that. It is pretty clear when a 3-4 year old wants to learn about numbers. She will sit and work with counting and grouping objects for extended periods. He may start pointing to written numerals and wanting to know what they mean. That is the time to start the sequence of activities in this book.

Allow your child all the time he needs to learn to count properly, to repeat favorite activities, and to use materials on her own, independently. Real mastery of math or anything else takes time, practice, and repetition. Moving a child along the sequence before she is ready will only cause problems, so err on the side of caution and make sure your child really understand each step before moving on. Have patience and allow this process to happen at its own rate.

Be positive

Shutterstock

When doing activities, avoid any hint of pressure, criticism, or negativity. Be totally positive and upbeat. Have fun! Early learning should always be a process of exploration, discovery, and achieving success through effort. Challenges are good; but allowing a child to become frustrated is definitely not.

If you see your child becoming frustrated with an activity, bring it to a positive conclusion and put it away for another day. Criticism, pressure, and other negative stressors have no place in early learning. Our children are in a unique and precious time of life, and require our unfailing love and support.

Always search for activities in your child's Learning Sweet Spot. Activities that are too difficult cause frustration. Those that are too easy cause boredom. These are the extremes you want to try to avoid. The best activities at any time are those that hold your child's attention, and that she wants to pursue even if she makes a few mistakes and does not master it right away. That is your child's Learning Sweet Spot.

If you see your child becoming frustrated with an activity, bring it to a positive conclusion and do something else. If your child is obviously bored because a material is too easy for him, move on to the next challenge.

Encourage your child's efforts

Discovery Moments blog (discoverymoments.com)

The habit of praising children constantly is not a real aid to their development. Repeatedly telling children how smart and wonderful they are is unnecessary. It can create children who assume everything will always fall into place for them because they are simply amazing people. When life doesn't work that way, they can become very frustrated! Praise is important and fine in small doses. Encouragement is even more effective.

Young children develop self-confidence and a positive self-image by mastering real skills and learning useful information. This helps children feel more in control of their environment. Helping your child accomplish this is perhaps the best way to help her develop a positive self-image based on real achievement instead of empty praise.

When a child finally masters a skill or understands something new, he experiences a tangible feeling of success. This experience, repeated many times in the early years with different materials, gives a child a positive sense of her capabilities that carries on for life. He welcomes new experiences because he has succeeded with so many already. This is the awesome power of early learning.

Samples of encouraging phrases to use include:

"You tried hard and didn't give up, way to go!"

"Keep trying, some things take time, you'll get it."

"Good try, keep working at it."

"You worked hard and figured it out, good job!"

"Give it your best."

"Nice work!"

"You really worked hard today!"

"Your work is getting better and better."

Allow time for repetition and independent work

We may think that if someone requires repetitions to learn something, they are not as smart as someone who 'gets it' right away. This definitely does not apply to young children. Children differ in how easily they master new skills; but all children benefit from repeating favorite activities.

It is during these repeated work sessions with materials that children are developing their brain architecture. Repetition strengthens brain nerve pathways. The efficiency and organization of these nerve pathways largely determine a child's intelligence. Let your child repeat favorite activities as often as he likes.

One goal of early learning is to create independent learners. Allow your child uninterrupted quiet time to work with materials independently. This is far more effective than to always be in 'teaching mode' with a child. Once you have demonstrated a material as described next, leave it out on your child's shelves for easy access. See pages 20 - 23 for more on displaying materials.

"The environment must be rich in motives which lend interest to activity and invite the child to conduct his own experiences."

Maria Montessori

Demonstrating materials

Montessori MOMents (mymontessorimoments.com)

When we show children a new activity or skill, it helps to demonstrate it. Our careful handling and enthusiasm for the material communicates to a child that it is a special item deserving of respect. Demonstrations with some materials, such as the cylinder block in the photo and others like the knobless cylinder, sorting, and transfer materials, can be done without saying a word. As Maria Montessori put it:

"Do not tell them how to do it. Show them how to do it and do not say a word. If you tell them, they will watch your lips move. If you show them, they will want to do it themselves."

When you demonstrate a material, move very slowly and carefully. Exaggerate your hand movements so your child can clearly see what you are doing. If there is a material, like rice or water, involved, always spill a little. Immediately stop and pick it up or clean up the spill. Provide a cloth and sponge so your child can do this for himself with water activities.

Using workbooks and worksheets

Most of us used worksheets in school, so we naturally think they are good tools for preschoolers. Superb worksheets are easily available online, making them quick and handy for time-challenged parents. I encourage you, however, not to begin with worksheets for your math activities.

Young children are acquiring a storehouse of sensory information about the real world through all of their senses, especially the sense of touch. A young child has a unique sensory and neuromuscular connection with her environment. Young children first learn best by handling and manipulating three dimensional objects and interacting with other people.

Between the ages of 3-6, children gradually use their accumulated sensory impressions of the world to start picturing the world mentally, using abstract thought. As this process progresses, we can then slowly introduce worksheets and workbooks, as well as high quality digital tablet apps.

Give your child plenty of experience with three dimensional objects first. When you see her becoming more comfortable working with letters, numbers, and flat shapes, you can gradually introduce worksheets, workbooks, and digital tablet apps.

The Three Step Lesson

The Three Step Lesson was developed by Maria Montessori. It is a very effective way of teaching children the names of shapes, colors, numerals, amounts, letter sounds, and many other things. The three steps move information from short term to long term memory. You can see an entire Three Step Lesson on amounts 1, 2, and 3 described starting on page 42.

Most Three Step Lessons use three objects. This is not a hard and fast rule. If using two objects works better, especially at first, use two. Your child will probably be able to 'graduate' to using three objects after a while. Here are the three steps:

Identify: tell the child the names of the objects, one at a time. *"This is one"*, *"This is two"*, etc.

Recognize: display all the objects, say their names, and ask your child to point to them. *"Show me where there is one"*, *"Show me where there are three"*, etc.

Remember: show the child each object, one at a time again, and ask your child to name it from memory. *"How many are here?"*, *"How many are here?"* etc.

Step two moves the information from short term to long term memory. We play different games in this step. For instance, once the child has named all the objects, have her close her eyes and switch the positions of the objects, then ask her to point to them as you name them again. Do this a few times. Put all the objects on a tabletop across the room and ask your child to go get each one as you ask for it. Repetition like this in step two helps get the information into long term memory.

Digital Math

Shutterstock

"The most important thing is a person, a person who incites your curiosity and feeds your curiosity; and machines cannot do this in the same way that people can." Steve Jobs

As the man responsible for the digital tablet explosion says, people are still our most important influences. Tablet apps, television, and video games can easily become electronic babysitters delivering mindless entertainment rather than useful educational tools. The keys are your involvement and taking a sensible approach to allowing children to use digital media.

The National Association for the Education of Young Children (NAEYC) has a paper you can download titled: Technology and Interactive Media as Tools in Early Childhood Programs Serving Children from Birth to Age 8 (naeyc.org/content/technology-and-young-children). They, and many pediatricians, recommend little or no tablet use for the first two years of a child's life. This is when children need to be using real object and interacting with the real world, not video screens.

Between the ages of 3-6, children gradually develop the capacity for abstract thought. One way to know when your child has developed significant abstract thinking ability is her level of interest in numbers and words. Math and reading use abstract line symbols to represent concrete objects, experiences, and ideas, which is the hallmark of abstract thought. When a child's brain is ready for abstract thought, an increased interest typically arises in words, numbers, and other abstract concepts. This is part of the natural flow of development.

The NAEYC recommends no more than 2 hrs. per day of screen time for 3-6 year olds. I would recommend a more conservative 1 hr. per day maximum. High quality educational tablet apps are a better choice for your child's screen time than passive television watching or video games.

Children typically enter sensitive periods for absorbing math and language during their late third and fourth years. This is when children are ready to gradually start using more abstract image and symbol-based materials, both on paper and on a tablet via good educational apps.

As a child demonstrates greater ability to learn about math and reading from 3 ½ - 5, high quality tablet apps can be gradually introduced. By the time a child is 5-6, tablet apps can be a regular part of a child's learning experiences, along with greater use of worksheets and workbooks which, like tablet apps, are more abstract than working with real objects.

From birth to 3 you should be reading with your child every day. One great way to introduce digital media in a positive way is to mix paper books with digital interactive tablet books during this period. This gets your child used to using a tablet and prepares him for using targeted educational apps later.

Get your child a small stylus when she starts using apps more often. A number of the apps include number writing practice; and a stylus helps prepare a child for writing more effectively than using a finger.

Good Apple and Android math apps are recommended throughout the math activities chapters in this book. These are apps that have the best features to help a young child absorb math concepts and develop number skills. I have tested hundreds of math and other preschool apps; and these are the ones that made the cut. Many apps fail to sequence math skills properly. They try to include a lot of content to increase their value, which is fine. Showing a child math challenges she has not been prepared for, however, such as switching quickly from counting up to ten to subtraction problems, is not effective.

Most of the math apps recommended in this book focus on specific skills. The ones that include options for different skill levels are noted, along with suggestions to optimize your child's use of each app.

If an app has an option to shut off the happy voices that constantly say, "*Sweet! Good job! You're great!*", please use it. These verbal reinforcements may seem like a good thing; but they are unnecessary. Children have a natural drive to learn, grow, and adapt. Too much outward reinforcement can train children to perform for verbal rewards rather than to satisfy their inner drive to develop.

Displaying learning materials

We display meaningful objects and photos on the walls and shelves of our homes. You can show the same respect for your child's learning materials. Rather than being tossed in a drawer or toy box, they can each have their own place on low shelves where your child can see them and have easy access. Displaying learning materials attractively this way shows that they are special, important items, deserving of everyone's respect.

Children react to materials differently when they are displayed this way. Each material clearly stands out as a unique attraction, which stimulates curiosity and helps children focus their attention right from the start as they get the material off the shelf. Returning it to the same spot completes a cycle of activity that teaches children to finish what they start. Here are some ideas:

"Education is a natural process carried out by the child and is not acquired by listening to words but by experiences in the environment."

Maria Montessori

Chasing Cheerios

Family Go Simple

Chasing Cheerios

The other essential for a home early learning area is a small table and chair:

Peaceful Parenting blog

"It is almost possible to say that there is a mathematical relationship between the beauty of his surroundings and the activity of the child; he will make discoveries rather more voluntarily in a gracious setting than in an ugly one."

Maria Montessori

When your child uses her materials, always have her follow through and reorganize and return each one to its place on the shelf. This will take reminders, and that's okay. Check your child's shelves regularly and make sure the materials look organized and ready for use. Involve your child in straightening up his shelves. This does not take long, and communicates to your child a sense of beauty order, and responsibility for her own things.

It is not hard to organize your kitchen and child's room to make everything child-sized and accessible. Use a stepstool for sink access, lower the clothing rod in the closet to child height, and place dishes and utensils on low shelves for easy access. Healthy snacks and juices can be placed on low shelves in cabinets and the refrigerator. Spice racks from Ikea make great book holders. Hang an analog clock (p. 98) and a simple calendar (p. 102) in your child's room. Hang a bulletin board at your child's eye level to pin up your child's drawings, sight words, a calendar, family photos, and other items. Magnets can be used with a metal dry erase board to post messages, sight words, and artwork.

Recommended Commercial Learning Materials

Many of the activities shown here are made using common, inexpensive items. A few high quality Montessori and other good learning materials will add greatly to the quality of your child's math experiences. Suggestions are given next for materials you can buy to complement those that you make. Having at least some of these will really accelerate your child's math learning.

The Montessori materials shown here cost under $200. These are high quality materials used in Montessori schools, and I highly recommend them. When your child has outgrown them you can sell them online and recover at least half of their cost. Following the Montessori materials are more commercial early learning materials with a math focus that I also recommend for parents who can afford them.

Diverting a portion of what you will otherwise spend on disposable plastic toys with no learning value to buying these wonderful materials for your child will greatly enhance her brain development.

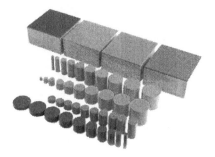

The **Montessori Knobless Cylinders** are a wonderful material for 3-5 year olds. They have the same four sets of ten cylinders as the Montessori Cylinder Blocks, without knobs and beautifully painted. They are used for size grading, counting, free building, and matching to graphic control cards. You can find these for around $60 at **Montessori Outlet** (montessorioutlet.com), an online supplier with quality materials at good prices.

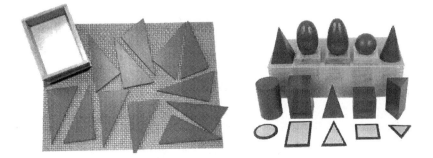

The **Montessori Blue Constructive Triangles** (left, above & p.82) are around $15, allow your child to explore making all kinds of geometric shapes and interesting figures. The **Montessori Geometric Solids** (right above & p.76), are expensive at around $60, but wonderful for giving children direct, hands-on experiences with the basic geometric shapes. See page 76 for less expensive alternatives that will also work for home use.

Safety Note: Montessori materials are made very precisely, with sharp corners, points, and edges. Be sure your child always uses them carefully to avoid injury. These materials should never be thrown or handled carelessly.

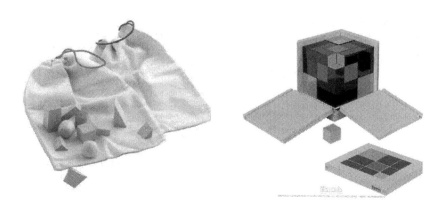

The **Mystery Bags & Geometric Shapes** (left, above and p.76) are an inexpensive and excellent material for learning the geometric shapes and educating a child's stereognostic sense – the ability to identify objects by touch. The **Montessori Trinomial Cube**, at around $40, is a very cool sensory and math material for 4-6 year olds that can be sold for at least $20-25 when your child is finished using it.

The **Montessori Sandpaper Numerals** (left, above and p.47, $7) and the **Teen Bead Bar Box** ($9, right, above and p.52) are wonderful and inexpensive math materials. Sandpaper numerals and letters really help children learn to use these graphic symbols. The bead bars are used for many of the activities with amounts larger than ten. These two materials, and the next Montessori materials shown, are highly recommended for your home math activities. These are the same materials used in Montessori schools with great results. Now, you will learn to use them at home. All materials are available at Montessori Outlet (montessorioutlet.com)

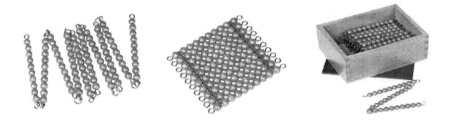

At left above: the **100 Golden Bead Chain** ($3, p.55). Middle: the **100 Golden Bead Square** ($4, p.55). Right: the **Box of 45 Golden Bead Ten Bars** ($16, p.55) These Montessori bead materials give your child hands-on experience with amounts up to 100. They are invaluable tools, used in many of the activities in this book. You can try making bead materials, but at a total cost of around $30 for all of the excellent, classroom quality bead materials illustrated here (including the bead bar box), why would you?

Above, the **Montessori Hundred Board** ($27, p.57). This is a very versatile material for illustrating the relationships between numbers. It is used for learning numerals 1-100, skip counting, squaring numbers, and more.

Montessori materials are not the only game in town. Next are more great materials that will complement and enhance your child's home early learning activities. Search by name on Amazon or at the suppliers listed:

Melissa & Doug Geometric Stacker. A great pre-math material for 2-3 year olds. It encourages counting and develops sensory discrimination.

Eureka Tub of Animal Counters. Early math activities use identical small objects. These fit the bill and come in a nice container for your child's shelves.

Left: **Melissa & Doug Wooden Shapes Sorting Clock**. Telling time is most easily learning with a simple analog clock, but this material is too versatile and good not to be on every child's shelves. It provides experiences with colors, shapes, numerals, counting, and of course, telling time. Right: **Melissa & Doug Pattern Blocks & Boards**. These are wonderful for exploring with plane (flat) shapes, symmetry, design, color, and visual – spatial recognition. Search Amazon for bigger sets if your child gets into these. You can download free pattern block design sheets from PreKinders at: prekinders.com/pattern-blocks.

Unifix Cubes are inexpensive, versatile, fantastic manipulative tools for grouping, counting, number operations, fractions, and seeing the relationships between amounts. I highly recommend them for preschoolers. Find these on Amazon. Cuisenaire Rods are also good pre-math tools; but I prefer rods composed of individual units, rather than assigning numerical values to solid rods based on their length. It is much clearer to a child when they see a rod with 5 separate blocks compared to one with 6. They can separate the individual blocks and reassemble them, which nicely reinforces math concepts.

The **Plan Toy Geometric Sorting Board,** at around $15, is a great introduction to geometric shapes, colors, and counting for a younger child. Give your young child plenty of time to work with these and the pre-math materials shown next. These and other early learning materials build all kinds of wonderful skills.

Recordkeeping

Keeping a simple record of your child's math activities can be very helpful. Children have periods of intense interest in different activities and experiences. Knowing what materials your child has used and was last using will help you keep her progressing through the sequence of math activities and skills.

The first time your child uses a new material, note the date and write in a capital 'I' for 'Introduced'. The next time, note the date of the second use of the material and write in a capital 'P' for 'Practicing'. When your child has truly mastered the information or skill the activity teaches, write in a capital 'M' for 'Mastered'.

There are record keeping sheets to print out in your set of free math printables (p.6). These also include Practical Life, Sensorial, and other early learning areas. Use just the math portion if you like, but getting your child involved in all these early learning areas is a great idea. Every area develops different vital skills and brain architecture. Read more about this at: www.montessorihomebook.com.

"It is true that we cannot make a genius. We can only give to each child the chance to fulfill his potential possibilities."

Maria Montessori

The Sequence of Math Activities

Doing math activities starts with pre-math skills development (p.30). Once these are in place, we have a clear first goal: learn all about amounts and numerals 0-100. As your child progresses toward this goal, other kinds of math activities are gradually introduced. This results in your child doing different types of activities during the same time period. This adds variety, and helps your child find something that interests him on any given day.

Here is how the Math Sequence in this book progresses:

1. **Developing pre-math skills**

2. **Learn amounts and numerals 0-10**

3. **Learn amounts and numerals 11-20**

4. **Learn amounts and numerals 31-100**

5. **While working towards 100, introduce addition and geometric shapes activities**

6. **Learn about the decimal system with numbers 101-1000**

7. **While working towards 1000, introduce multiplication, fractions, subtraction, division, and practical skills like learning to tell time and using a calendar**

This sequence of activities, pursued for at least a year before your child enters school, will give her an excellent foundation of math skills. Your child should experience quick success with math in school, which is a great predictor of future success. Getting a head start like this is the best preparation you can give your child.

"To assist a child we must provide him with an environment which will enable him to develop freely."

"Free choice is one of the highest of all the mental processes."

Maria Montessori

Developing Pre-Math Skills

Chasing Cheerios blog

These activities prepare a child for math. To be successful with number activities, a young child needs to be able to:

Visually focus on and handle individual objects in groups

Learn to carefully count objects in different groups

Understand the concept of 1 : 1 Correspondence

Visually focus on specific line symbols (letters and numerals)

Execute a writing grasp

Pre-math skills are developed by with simple activities, mostly using hands-on materials, when a child is 2-4 years old. Do many of these activities on a regular basis before your child starts the math activities that follow. Leaving out this important step can result in less than optimal progress with the math activities to come.

If you are starting with a 4-6 year old, don't leave these activities out and go right to the 0-100 activities! Present many of the pre-math materials and see which ones your child gets into. The Transfer materials (p.35) are especially useful for developing a writing grasp. If the pasta and other object-based Sorting activities (p.31) are too easy, try the metal washers and straws length sorting materials, as well as sorting pictures and shapes.

Your child's interest is always your best guide to which of these activities to do and when. Try different ones, looking for sparks of spontaneous interest and focused attention. Encourage that spark to grow as if it is a rare, delicate flower.

When you see that a material attracts and holds your child's attention, let him work with it as long as she likes on her own. Allow quiet time for this work. This is how young children develop the ability to concentrate, which develops inner self-discipline and the ability to learn anything.

The following are good activities and apps for helping your child develop these important pre-math skills. Try many of them to see which ones your child really gets into. Place the hands-on materials on your child's shelves for easy access.

Sorting

Sorting materials are great for developing brain architecture and pre-math skills. Sorting gives a child the satisfaction of creating ordered groups from random chaos. These materials are easy to set up and can be varied in all kinds of interesting ways to meet your child's interests and skill level. Sorting materials develop:

- **The ability to visually discriminate between differences and similarities**
- **The concept of discrete groups**
- **Hand and finger muscle control and coordination**
- **Counting skills**
- **Concentration skills**
- **Confidence and a positive self-image**

As in the coins sorting photo, the basic setup is a central container with a collection of different objects, surrounded by separate smaller containers for sorting the objects according to their characteristics: shape, size, color, etc.

The following are examples of good sorting materials, many of which are used in Montessori and other good preschools. They are easy and fun to use at home, too. Feel free to try variations and different materials. Sorting can be modified in many ways based on what you have available.

Top: **Sorting coins**. A central container is surrounded by identical smaller ones for sorting. Vary this by including just 10 of each coin and encourage counting to 10 while sorting.

Second: **Sorting colors**. Paint color chips in different shades of red, yellow, and blue are sorted by color. Include more colors & shades when your child is ready.

Peaceful Parenting blog

Third: **Sorting wooden beads**. The beads are identical except for their colors. Kitchen tongs used to pick up the beads add a fine muscle control challenge that helps a child work toward developing a writing grasp (p.35)

Bottom: **Sorting metal washers by size**. Using washers that are very close in size adds to the challenge. Use 10 of each size to encourage counting, and perhaps a toothpick for picking up the washers.

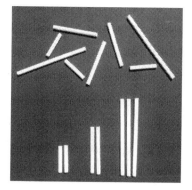

The straw sorting material in the photo increases the difficulty when a child is ready for more challenge. Cut straws into 3", 5", and 7" lengths. Make at least 5 of each length. Lay them out in a random group. Show your child how to place the shortest straws on the left, lined up like soldiers, and increasingly longer groups to the right. Your child can leave space between the groups or bring them all together. This encourages left to right tracking for reading.

Here is a way to help your child at first. Looking at the random group, ask your child, *"Can you find all the shortest straws?"* Show him one if needed. Once these are all found and lined up in a group, ask your child to find the shortest straws in the random group again. Repeat as each group is found and lined up. For the last group, say, *"These are the longest straws."*

You can increase the difficulty by cutting the straws in lengths that are closer together, and adding more lengths. For instance, cut 5 each of straws that are 1", 2", 3", 4", etc., all the way up to 10" long.

The bottom photo on the previous page shows another good sorting experience that prepares a child for math. Use colored wooden beads sorted by color. Start with five colors. Include 1 bead of one color in the group, 2 beads of the next color, 3 of the next, 4 of the next, and 5 beads of the last color.

Your child now sorts the beads by colors and counts how many are in each group. Each group of beads can also be laid end to end to give a visual comparison of their relative sizes.

Next, use ten colors of beads and make ten groups of from 1-10 beads in each and repeat the activity. This reinforces amounts up to ten and teaches careful counting.

Encourage Careful Counting

When your child has grouped the straws by length or the washers by size, encourage her to carefully count the objects in each group. Make sure there are no more than 10 in each group. It is best to start with 5 and work up to 10.

Children should count by touching the objects in turn and saying the numbers. They often get their touching of the objects out of synch with their counting.

Careful counting is done by saying each number *exactly* when the child's finger touches each object.

Help your child slow down and count carefully, saying each number, "*One, two, three,* " etc., exactly when his finger touches each object. Give your child lots of practice doing this. Learning to count carefully insures that your child will be accurate with all her later math work.

Here are more sorting ideas:

different shapes of pasta

colored foam pom poms from a crafts store moved with tweezers

different kinds of beans picked up with a small spoon

colored rubber bands picked up with a toothpick or tweezers

pictures of animals and things that live on air, land , and water

pictures of birds, fish, insects, mammals, reptiles, and crustaceans

Good iPad sorting apps include:

Sort It Out

Smart Fish Matrix

Simple Sort

Transfers

Young children love moving various materials and colored water back and forth between containers. The materials can be easily varied to provide easier or more difficult challenges. Spills are to be expected, so have a sponge and cloth ready and show your child how to stop and pick up objects or clean spills.

Transfers encourage the gradual development of a proper writing grasp, as shown in the activity photos. This won't happen overnight, so allow plenty of time and practice for your child to master each more sophisticated grasp in turn.

A proper writing grasp. The instrument is held lightly between the thumb and first finger, with the other fingers curled underneath for support. The Transfer materials progress from a whole hand grasp to using a writing grasp to hold a small spoon. Skills developed with Transfer materials include:

Visual recognition. The child must accurately visualize the containers, the tool, and how each transfer will be accomplished.

Concept of 1:1 Correspondence. Transfers that involve one spot for one object help teach this critical math concept.

Small muscle control and coordination. These activities gradually train the fingers to execute a writing grasp so that your child will be able to write numbers later.

Careful counting. See p.34.

Functional independence skills. These activities help children learn how to pour their own juice and other drinks by themselves. They learn how to use simple tools, and how to clean up solid and liquid spills.

Here is a sequence of Transfer materials that take a child gradually from an early, whole hand grasp all the way to a proper writing grasp:

The top photo shows a child moving water back and forth with a small sponge. This exercises the whole hand grasp and uses water, which children love. Dry materials could also be moved by hand this way.

Chasing Cheerios blog

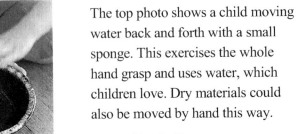

In the middle photo, a child uses a turkey baster to move water between two containers. The bulb is squeezed using either a whole hand or 'C' shaped grasp. Learning how to draw up and expel the water adds another challenge to master.

Chasing Cheerios blog

In the bottom photo, rice is poured back and forth between small cups. This uses a 'C' shaped grasp, preparing a child for the opposing thumb grasps used in the next transfer materials.

Top: pouring rice or beans between two pitchers with handles and pouring lips adds the new challenge of using the lips and rotating the wrist to pour. Next, adding water increases the difficulty and prepares a child for pouring her own drinks.

Second: Moving plastic practice golf balls between egg carton compartments using kitchen tongs. Now, the thumb opposes all four fingers, preparing the child for a writing grasp. This material also teaches 1:1 Correspondence, a vital math concept.

Third: Another 1:1 Correspondence material, using crafts pom poms placed with tweezers on the suction cups of an overturned soap holder.

The Education of Ours

Bottom: Moving water colored with food coloring between small cups with an eyedropper. Now, two fingers are opposed to the thumb, refining the grasp further towards a writing grasp.

These activities lead up to using a small measuring spoon – usually the smallest – to move small beans or rice, as in the next photo. Moving through this entire sequence, with plenty of practice, prepares a child for writing numerals.

A tiny spoon requires close to a true writing grasp

Bead Threading

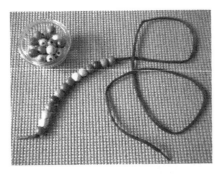

Threading colored wooden beads is a great pre-math and small muscle activity. Start with beads that are the same size and shape, differing only in color. These are available at most crafts stores. Tie a knot in one end of a shoelace and let your child freely play with threading them on. Next, introduce counting the beads as your child threads them on, focusing on counting up to ten.

Color patterns are another good activity. Make a 'master' pattern first on the shoelace by threading on 5-10 beads in a sequence of different colors. Now, your child repeats the pattern. You can also draw colored circles on cards as the master pattern for your child to match.

"These words reveal the child's inner needs; 'Help me to do it alone'."

Maria Montessori

Marbles & Golf Tees

For this fun activity you need a block of floral foam, golf tees, and marbles. Put the marbles and tees in separate bowls, and put it all on a nice tray for your child's shelves.   *Photo: Pink & Green Mama blog*

Let your child freely explore with pressing the tees in and balancing marbles on them. Resist the urge to jump in and show your child how well *you* can do it. With practice, children figure out how to insert the tees straight so that the marbles stay on.

Once he has done this awhile, encourage your child to make a straight line of 1-10 tees and marbles and count them, left to right. Always encourage counting objects in a line left to right, as this prepares a child's visual tracking for reading.

Unifix Cubes

Unifix Cubes (p.27) are a wonderful manipulative for preparing your child for math as well as learning specific math skills. Your child can freely explore with them at first. Then, introduce counting connected rods of up to 10 cubes. Included in your free Math Printables (p.6), is a Unifix Cubes to dots matching activity that makes another great early math experience.

Montessori Knobless Cylinders

This classic Montessori material, shown on p.24, is wonderful for developing early math skills. Children get most of what they need from it just by exploring and experimenting with the four groups of ten cylinders each.

Amounts & Numerals 0-100

Your child should by now have used a number of the pre-math materials in the previous section. He should have been exposed to grouping and careful counting of up to 10 objects. Ideally, she is now showing an increased interest in numbers and counting. If your child has not had these experiences, return to the pre-math materials and provide this important foundation. If your child is counting well and has had this background, it is time to move on. The 0-100 activities all follow a similar pattern:

1. **Learn the amounts by themselves**
2. **Learn the numerals by themselves**
3. **Match the amounts with the numerals**

To make it easier, we break up the process into stages: 0-10, 11-20, 21-30, 31-40, etc, up to 100. This is how children develop a firm foundation of math understanding. Going too fast or leaving out steps can result in gaps in your child's math understanding. All this work early on will pay off later.

For our objects, we can use any small identical objects. Coins work perfectly, and since we will be doing coin exchange activities soon, now is a great time to introduce them. If you use coins for these first activities, use only one kind, usually pennies or quarters. Quarters are larger and more impressive. Other suitable objects include identically sized and colored poker chips, Lego pieces, or even lima beans. Other materials you will need for these activities include:

- **0-10 and 11-100 Numeral Cards from the free Math Printables** (p.6)
- **Small cups and straws**
- **Montessori Sandpaper Numerals** (p.25)
- **Cornmeal and a shallow pan**
- **Montessori Teen Bead Bar Box** (p.26)
- **Unifix Cubes** (p.27)
- **Objects for tracing** (p.47, 79-81)
- **Montessori Hundred Board** (p.26)

Amounts & Numerals 0-10

We start a child's journey into math by learning amounts 0-10 using Three Step Lessons (p.17) with groups of from 1-10 identical objects. Since these lessons are best done with three objects or items, we do 1-3 first, then 4-6, then 7-10. Quarters or pennies are perfect for these lessons. They are identical in size, color, and weight. Children love to handle money. It is also easy to gather up to 34 of either when you do Three Step Lessons with groups of 7, 8, 9, and 10.

"Is it really necessary to go through every single step in the sequence?"

Because mathematics follows a very logical sequence, from small numbers up to infinitely large numbers, and including operations with numbers, geometry, fractions, etc, following the sequence of activities is the best way to insure that your child has a firm math foundation to build on.

With that said, children are all different in how they learn, how much repetition is required, and in their pace of learning. Tune in to how your child and go with the flow. Some activities and concepts will be learned more quickly than others. Follow your child's lead and interest level. Nothing is gained by pressuring a young child to learn. Make it fun!

Every time you introduce a new concept, test your child's memory of those learned before. Identify areas needing extra time and provide it. If your child gets something quickly and seems bored repeating it, it is okay to move on. If she gets frustrated, you are probably going a bit too fast. Having fun, exploring new skills, and developing a positive confidence built on success with the activities are your goals. Start with zero:

Zero

Lay out a mat as if you are preparing to do a Three Step Lesson. Tell your child, *"We are going to do a very special number today."* Point to the empty mat and say, *"This is zero. Zero means none, or nothing."*

Ask your child to point to zero, hand you zero, and bring you zero. Show your child your empty hand and ask, *"How many are here?"* Show your child an empty bowl and ask, *"How many oranges are in the bowl?"* Play many similar games like this. Help if needed so your child learns that zero means none, or nothing.

Learning Amounts 1, 2, & 3

Start by doing Three Step Lessons with 1, 2, and 3 identical objects. Here are all three steps, using quarters for objects:

Step one: Identify

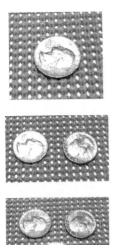

Top: set out one quarter and say, "*This is one.*" Child holds, looks at object, and says "*One.*"

Middle: remove the one, set out two, and say, "*This is two.*" Count the objects, "*One, two.*" Child counts objects and repeats, "*This is two, One, two.*"

Bottom: Lay out three and say, "*This is three. One, two, three.*" Child repeats as above.

Step two: Recognize

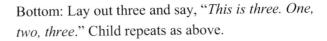

Top: lay out all three groups. Ask, "*Show me where there is one.*" Child points to the single object. "*Where are three?*" Child points to three objects. "*Where are two?*" Child points to two objects.

Bottom: Have your child close her eyes while you change the arrangement of the groups. Your child opens her eyes and you repeat the above sequence.

Do many different arrangements this way.

Step three: Remember

Set out each group by itself, as in step one, and ask your child, "*How many are here?*" With each group. If the information has made it into your child's long term memory, he will remember the groups correctly.

One of the most helpful tips for a successful Three Step Lesson: spend the most time in step two. Changing the arrangements a number of times and having your child count and identify the groups is what moves the information from short term to long term memory. If three objects seems a bit much at first with your child, use two and progress to using three later when he has the hang of it.

If you get to either step two or three and your child cannot identify of remember the amounts, just start over at step one, and play more games in step two. If that doesn't do it, your child is either not really interested that day or not ready to learn the amounts. Bring the activity to a positive conclusion and try again another day. No worries, no stress, everything will happen in time.

Learning amounts 4-10

When your child easily recognizes, counts, and makes groups of 1, 2, and 3 objects, do Three Step Lessons with groups of 4, 5, and 6 objects. Review amounts of 1, 2, and 3 objects while you do this.

When your child consistently recognizes groups of 4, 5, and 6 objects, do Three Step Lessons with groups of 7, 8, 9, and 10 objects. Review amounts of from 1-6 objects while you do this.

This takes varying amounts of time with each child. The important thing is to keep it fun and make sure your child truly masters recognizing and making groups of from 1-10 identical objects.

Three Step Lesson alternatives

The Three Step Lesson is a great teaching tool, used in Montessori schools all over the world. It can be used to teach a child the names of all kinds of things. It is not foolproof, however, and some children learn more effectively by other means. Next are some good alternatives to Three Step Lessons for learning to recognize groups of from 1-10 objects.

Top: Exchanging coins. This is a natural activity that children like. Show your child that 5 pennies = 1 nickel, 10 pennies = 1 dime, as do 2 nickels. Exchange these coins back and forth with each other all kinds of ways, encouraging careful counting.

Second photo: Straws and cups. Use identical small cups, like Dixie cups or similar, and straws cut in half. Start with an empty cup for zero and gradually work your way up to counting out from 1-10 straws into separate cups. Practice counting groups of straws by themselves. A nice extension is to rubber band the groups together.

Next photos: Unifix Cubes (p.27). Make groups of 1-10 cubes for your child to carefully count and identify. Test her knowledge by handing her rods built with varying numbers of cubes to identify. Encourage your child to make a graded arrangement of rods with from 1-10 cubes, as in the second photo. In the math printables you will find a Unifix Cubes to Dots Matching activity.

Bottom: The 1-9 bead bars from the Montessori Teen Bead Bar Box (p. 25) are great for counting and identifying amounts from 1-10. You will need these for the next activities, so get them now. The box costs around $8.

Use coins, bead bars, Unifix Cubes, or other objects to do many greater than and less than problems. Write out cards as in the photo and review what they mean with your child. Encourage him to count to determine which sign to place between the groups of objects or bead bars.

Other good ways of introducing and reinforcing amounts of from 1-10 are playing dominoes and rolling dice. Dominoes is a classic game with many options as your child gets older. Start with a double six or a double nine set. When your child is ready, graduate to a double fifteen set. A simple pair of dice make another great math material. Play games rolling the dice and counting the dots on each, and their total. Have your child draw pictures of how the dots appear on the dice. Later, your child can match numerals with the dots on the dice.

Good iPad dominoes apps include Dominoes HD and Domino Kids Calculations. Good Android dominoes apps include Dominos Live and Dominoes Game.

Mancala, pictured above, is one of the oldest games in the world, and wonderful for teaching counting and grouping objects, as well as strategy. You can find Mancala games at most toy stores, an also play online.

Good first math apps

When your child starts learning amounts 0-10, it is also time to introduce high quality digital tablet math apps. Here are ideas for apps that your child will use for a good period of time while learning math.

iPad

Intro to Math

Dominos Easy Match

Farm 123

Learn Money: Counting Coins and Bills

Montessori Numberland HD

Montessori Numbers – Math Activities for Kids

Learn to Count Numbers 1-10

Bugs and Numbers

Android

Farm 123

Bugs and Buttons

Kindergarten Kids Math

Monkey Math School Sunshine

Toddler Counting 123 HD

Count Up To Ten

Whether you use Three Step Lessons or the alternative activities, the goal is the same: help your child learn to quickly and correctly identify and count groups of from 1-10 objects. As he is working on this, you can also start with the next activities for learning the numerals 0-10. Working on these will add variety and choice to your activities. The final step comes on p.49-51, when your child matches amounts and numerals 0-10. Then, we move right on into the larger numbers 11-100.

Learning the numerals 0-10

Your child has learned or is working on amounts 1-10. Now you can separately introduce the numerals 0-10. This prepares your child for the final step of matching the amounts and numerals. While your child is learning the numerals, she should also be learning to write them. For these activities, you will need:

Left: Montessori Sandpaper Numerals. These give tactile, visual, and auditory impressions. **Middle**: a shallow tray with cornmeal for practicing tracing numerals. **Right:** objects for tracing. Pictured is the excellent, inexpensive ($8) Primary Shapes Template Set from Learning Resources. You can also use plastic cookie cutters, wooden numerals and letters from a crafts store, and objects around your house that your child can trace.

Sandpaper numerals give your child simultaneous tactile, visual, and auditory sense impressions. Your child traces the numeral with the first two fingers while looking at it and saying its name. This multi-sensory experience really helps get information into a young child's brain, while also creating muscle memory for writing.

A shallow pan with a thin layer of cornmeal is perfect for practicing writing. A quick shake of the pan 'erases' the letter or numeral. Using an unsharpened pencil to write the numerals in the cornmeal adds the element of using a writing instrument, making the activity even more valuable.

Drawing and tracing are perfect for developing writing skills. Make sure your child always has access to drawing materials like colored pencils, markers, crayons, and large drawing pads. Materials like the shapes templates in the photo allow simultaneous experience with tracing, which prepares for writing, and also with basic shapes and geometry.

There are many great tablet apps for learning to write letters and numerals. Since most children are becoming interested in learning to read and write around the same time they learn about numbers, here are good math apps for practicing letter and number writing:

iPad writing apps

Montessori Letter Sounds

Write On

Approach To Montessori: Numbers

Letter School.

Android writing apps

Writing Numbers

Kids Handwriting Grade K

Phonics and Handwriting

Magic Slate HD for Tablets

Get your child a stylus like the Mini Alloy Stylus. Encourage your child to use the stylus instead of his finger when writing. Using a finger does not develop writing skill. As your child learns the numerals and continues on with her math activities, make sure she is also practicing writing the numerals, writing out addition and other problems, on paper so that her writing skills parallel her number skills development.

The numerals 0-10 are learned by using the sandpaper numerals in a series of Three Step Lessons when you show your child the numerals in Step One, have her trace the numeral with two fingers while looking at it and saying its name. Also, give your child a chance to 'write' each numeral in the cornmeal tray as he learns them. Here is a Three Step Lesson review, using the sandpaper numerals:

Identify

Show your child the zero. Trace it slowly with the first two fingers of your right hand as you look at it and say, "Zero". Your child repeats what you did.

Repeat this with the 1 and the 2.

Recognize

Lay out all three numerals – the 0, 1, and 2. Ask your child to point to them as you name them. Have your child close his eyes and rearrange the numerals differently. Again ask your child to point to the numerals as you name them. Repeat this a few times.

Remember

As in the first step, show your child the numerals one at a time again. Ask her what each one says. If the information moved into your child's long term memory, she will remember. If not, start over in step one, as long as your child is willing and interested. It may take multiple lessons for your child to master the numerals.

Keep the cornmeal tray handy and let your child practice writing each numeral in it in Step One and whenever he wants to. If your child has not fully developed a writing grasp yet provide the Transfer (p.35-38) materials, and also encourage drawing and tracing, as discussed earlier. All these activities promote the development of a writing grasp.

When your child knows 0, 1, and 2 well, do 3, 4, and 5. When all these are mastered, do 7, 8, 9, and 10.

When your child has completed learning about amounts and numerals 0-10 separately, it is time to match them up!

Matching amounts & numerals 0-10

Now your child completes the process by matching up the amounts and numerals he has learned. This is a big step, so high fives are in order! Encouraging your child at every step of the learning process is important. If your child has written numerals or done drawings with numbers on them, put these up on her wall and on your fridge. Make a big deal about your child learning number skills. This communicates that these are big achievements in your family, deserving of respect and admiration. To match up amounts and numerals 0-10, we use a few simple activities.

Straws & Cups

You can make this material for $2-3, less if you already have cups and straws. All you need are 11 identical small cups, such as Dixie cups or similar, 55 straws cut about 4" long, and the 0-10 Numeral Cards from your Math Printables (p.6). A nice tray makes it easy to display this material on your child's shelves. Have your child bring the tray to a table. Show him how to set up the cups and numerals as shown in the next photo. Let him take over when he wants to.

Point to the zero and ask your child how many straws to put there. She should know the answer – none. Count out one straw and put it in the 1 cup. Let your child take over and finish, ending like this:

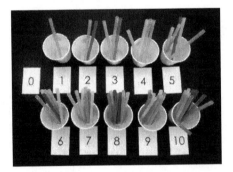

A nice extension is to bind each group together with a rubber band, further reinforcing the concept of objects in groups. You can also use coins or other objects, which leads nicely into the next activity.

Cards & Counters

For this activity, you need the numeral cards and 55 pennies or other identical coins. Pennies are good because they reinforce the concept of one, which will come in handy for the coming activities using larger amounts. Here is the layout:

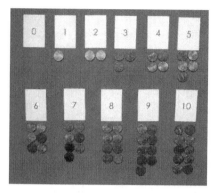

Show your child how to lay the pennies out as shown, in sets of two, counting as he goes. This also makes it easy to see even numbers, where each penny has a partner, and odd numbers, where the last penny stands alone. Zero is neither an even nor an odd number. This activity can also be done using Unifix Cubes or Montessori 1-10 bead bars:

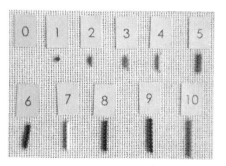

Montessori Print Shop, a great online source for printables, has excellent graphic materials for this activity. Check out their 1-10 Counting Cards, and the 0-10 Numbers and Counters. Each is under a dollar. You can also make your own using the product images as a guide.

When your child has worked with these activities and is very good at counting, identifying, and matching amounts and numerals 0-10, it is time to move on to amounts and numerals 11-20.

Amounts & Numerals 11-20

Now we repeat the same sequence used for 0-10 for amounts and numerals 11-20: learn the amounts, learn the numerals, and match the amounts and numerals. Once your child gets to 21-100, we can streamline the process a bit.

For these activities, you need the 11-20 Numeral Cards from your math printables (p.6), and the Montessori Teen Bead Bar Box (p.25). This great material costs only $7 at the time of this writing from Montessori Outlet online. If your child has worked enough with exchanging coins to truly understand that one dime = ten pennies, you can also use coins. The bead bars show the amounts more clearly. Here is how amounts larger than 10 are made using bead bars:

A ten bar and a four bar, laid end to end, makes 14. When you do this, say, *"Ten and four makes fourteen."* Give your child a sharp pencil, or a toothpick to use for doing careful counting with the bead bars. Make sure she touches each bead and says the number at the same time so that her counting stays accurate.

Start with Three Step Lessons with amounts 11, 12, and 13, using bead bars. You can also use dimes and pennies if your child truly understands that one dime = ten pennies. At left below, three dimes are ready to match up with 1, 2, and 3 pennies to make 11, 12, and 13, as at right:

When your child can easily count and accurately identify amounts of 11, 12, and 13, do Three Step Lessons with 14, 15, and 16. Once these are mastered, do 17, 18, 19, and 20.

To learn the numerals 11-20, start again with 11, 12, and 13, using the 11-20 Numeral Cards from the math printables (p.6).

"Ten and one __says__ eleven"

Do Three Step Lessons with 11, 12, and 13, and then the rest of the numerals 14-20, as with the amounts.

Matching amounts and numerals 11-20

Here are the layouts for matching these up. These photos show 11-15:

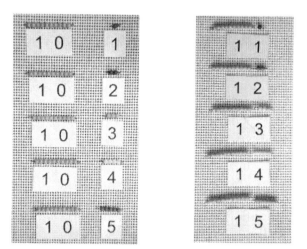

This layout can be used for amounts and numerals all the way to 100. Here is how you move from the layout on the left to the one on the right:

Start with 10 and 1 at the top of the left layout. Put the bead bars together, saying, *"Ten and one makes eleven."* Now, put the numeral cards together under the bars, saying, *"Ten and one says eleven."* Let your child take over whenever he likes and finish combining the bars and numeral cards. Encourage counting to verify amounts. Do another layout for 16-20.

When you get to 20, make a big deal out of that number. We use a ten-based number system, so it helps to reinforce that at 20, 30, 40, etc. You can do layouts, like these for example:

Amounts & Numerals 21-100

By the time most children get here, it is okay to dispense with the Three Step Lessons and make amounts and numerals at the same time. You can certainly continue doing lessons at least through 30-40 if needed, do what is best for your child. Most of the time kids start to see the repeating pattern of ten in our number system, so the main thing they need to learn is the 20, 30, 40, 50, etc., sequence as they go up to 100.

Larger numbers are done using the same layout shown on p.53 for 11-15. Here is a sample layout for starting amounts and numerals in the thirties:

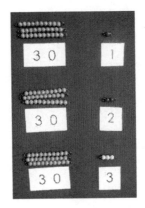

These layouts can all be done using dimes and pennies if that's how you and your child started out. When you get into larger numbers using bead bars, you will need the Montessori box of 45 golden bead ten bars (p.26) in order to have enough ten bars. By the time you are in the fifties, you may find your child can move a bit faster, as he will probably have the pattern down.

As you work towards 100, test your child's memory of numbers she has worked with. Lay out an amount like 25 using bead bars, and have your child make the correct numeral for that amount. Next, lay out a numeral, like 43, and have your child build that amount next to it. Do this with many different numbers. You will quickly see if your child needs a bit more practice.

> While working towards 100, you can also start Operations with Numbers (p.68), Geometric Shapes (p.76), and Fractions (p.84) activities. Mix these during the same time period based on your child's interest level. This adds variety and gives your child options for what to do on a given day. Regular reviews help. Always use your child's interest and enthusiasm as your guide.

When your child reaches 100

Reaching 100 is a big deal! Now, your child uses new materials to reinforce the relationship between all the numbers she has learned. These include the Montessori 100 Golden Bead Chain (left) and Hundred Square (right):

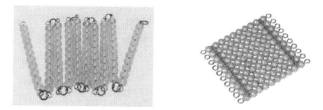

Together, these cost about $5 at Montessori Outlet online. They are invaluable tools for helping a young child see how objects in groups of ten interact and build to create larger numbers. Next are activities your child can do with these materials.

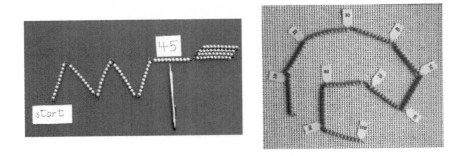

Left: Write a numeral (or use numeral cards) and show it to your child. Your child starts at the left end (left to right tracking for reading) and counts up to that numeral. He lays the counter pointing toward that bead and places the numeral card above. Your child can bend each bar of ten beads leading up to the numeral, and learn to count by tens and units: "*Ten, twenty, thirty, forty, forty one, forty two, forty three, forty four, forty five.*" Do many different numbers this way. You can also point to a specific bead and have your child count up to it

Right: Print and cut out the 100 Golden Bead Chain Pointers from the math printables (p.6). Your child counts the chain and places the pointers where they belong. This reinforces the even ten numbers.

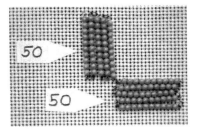

Another good activity is to bunch groups of ten bars on the chain together and make pointers with numerals showing how many are in each group. In the photo, the chain has been divided evenly into two groups of 50 each. Make all the different pairs of groups possible: 10/90, 20/80, 70/30, 40/60, 50/50. Reinforce with your child that each of these pairs equals 100.

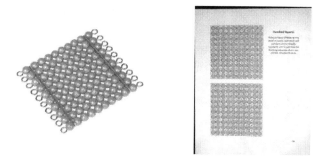

Let your child count the beads on the Hundred Square (left) to verify that there are 100. Print out the Hundred Squares from your math printables (right), and have your child count the gold circles on one of these to verify that they also have 100. This will help your child transition to using the printed hundred squares to represent 100 in the coming decimal system and large number activities.

The Hundred Board

When your child gets well into amounts and numerals in the 20's or 30's, she can start using the Hundred Board. This versatile material costs about $27 at Montessori Outlet online. It really helps children understand the relationships between numbers in our 10-based, decimal number system.

Montessori Print Shop offers an alternative, the printable 1-100 Math Series, which, at under $3, includes printables for skip counting and other activities. Check the web site at: montessoriprintshop.com

Tablet apps are great for Hundred Board activities. Good iPad apps include:

Hundred Board

100's Board

Skip Counting

Montessori Bead Skip Counting

There are great free hundred board materials online at these url's:

livingmontessorinow.com/2014/01/21/100th-day-activities-free-printable-extensions-for-the-hundred-board

abcya.com/interactive_100_number_chart.htm

mathwire.com/100board/hbpuzzles.pdf

Activities with the Hundred Board

Top: The first activity most children do is fill the board spaces with pennies or other identical objects, starting at the top left and filling each row left to right horizontally, counting from 1-100.

Bottom: Next, fill the spaces using the numerals, again starting at 1 and progressing to 100 to fill the board.

Point out how all the numerals in each vertical row end in the same numeral, and practice counting the numerals in the vertical rows from the top down.

Here are more Hundred Board ideas:

- Give your child numerals at random at have him find their correct place on the board.

- Hand your child random amounts made using bead bars, such as 38, and have her find the correct numeral for the amount, and place the numeral in the correct place on the Hundred Board.

- Your child fills the board with every other numeral tile, starting with 1, to create a board of odd numbers. Repeat, starting at 2, to create a board with all the even numbers. Have your child count each board start to finish.

- Do variations of the above activity by counting the board and placing every third tile (3, 6, 9, 12, etc), every fourth tile (4, 8, 12, 16, etc), every fifth tile, and so on, up to every tenth tile. Help your child as needed to count each board start to finish. This introduces skip counting. Good iPad apps for this: Skip Counting, and Montessori Bead Skip Counting.

- After your child fills the board with numeral tiles, have her close her eyes. Remove 5-10 of the tiles at random and lay them next to the board. Your child opens her eyes and finds the proper place for each of the missing tiles and replaces them on the board.

- Print out the Hundred Board from your math printables (p.6). Give your child the printout and a highlighter. Start with 1, and call out one of the numerals that touch the one – either 2, 11, or 12. Your child makes a line from the 1 to that numeral. Continue this way, working your way all over the board.

- Introduce your child to the concept of squaring numbers:

The photo on the left on the previous page shows 2 squared. The photo on the right shows 5 squared. Do many numbers this way, helping your child as needed to understand the different counting required.

To prepare your child for larger numbers and the decimal system, use the Hundred Board and other materials to make 100 in different ways:

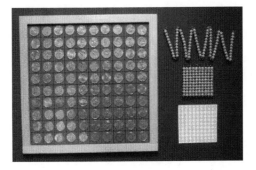

Above, 100 made using pennies on the Hundred Board, the 100 Golden Bead Chain and Square, and a printed 100 square from the path printables. This reinforces what 100 is. To save time, have your child verify that each row contains 10 on the board and the Hundred Square, and then skip count the rows by tens: 10, 20, 30, etc. If your child has used coins and truly understands that there are 10 pennies in a dime, you can use 10 dimes with this layout. Similarly, you can lay out a nickel on every fifth square on the board and then skip count from 5-100 by fives.

You can find many excellent Hundred Board printables to use at home at: donnayoung.org/math/100-number.htm

"Only through freedom and environmental experience is it practically possible for human development to occur."

"The child builds his inmost self out of the deeply held impressions he receives."

Maria Montessori

The Decimal System

With the next activities, your child gradually works up to amounts and numerals up to 1000. As we get into the larger numbers, we start learning the place values of the decimal system: units, tens, hundreds, thousands, etc.

While your child is working on larger numbers, he can also be working on Operations with Numbers (p.68), and Geometric Shapes (p.76). Mixing up these activities adds variety and maintains high interest. Work with whatever activities your child is into on any given day. Make them all available on low shelves for easy access.

Equipment

For these activities, you will need the materials you have used so far, as well as the Decimal System Numerals and Place Value Card from the Math Printables (p.6). You will also need a stapler and a black marker.

Other resources

The Hundred Board 101-200 iPad app can help your child move into larger numbers. Good iPad apps to use to teach your child the decimal system include: Montessori Place Value, and Stamp Game.

Montessori Print Shop offers a wonderful free material, the Printable Stamp Game and Instructions. For decimal system activities and making larger numbers, their free Large Number Cards are also excellent.

Making Numbers

Set out the cards and amounts for making 164:

As you put the amounts together, say, " *One hundred plus sixty plus four makes one hundred sixty four.*" Then put the numerals together and say, "*One hundred, sixty, and four says one hundred sixty four*":

Do many numbers from 100-199 in this way. Test your child's knowledge of making both amounts and numerals. Give your child different amounts and let her make their numerals, and vice versa. As your child's understanding grows, he can do both steps independently when you simply say a number from 100-199. Encourage your child to write the numbers she makes. When your child is ready to move into the 200's, simply introduce another printed Hundred Square:

Make many numbers from 200-300, and then move through all the hundreds in sequence, to 999. Observe how your child responds. If you see that he is truly understanding this process well, you can move a bit faster when you get into larger numbers. As you did with numbers from 1-100, periodically test your child's understanding by making an amount at random and having her make the correct numeral for it, and vice versa.

Once your child gets to 1000, it is time to reinforce this new placeholder and introduce the other placeholders of the decimal system for numbers your child has worked with so far: units, tens, and hundreds.

Making 1000

A great project for giving your child concrete experience with 1000 objects starts with a bag of bulk crafts beads, identical in size, shape, and color. Get a roll of string and some electrical tape in two colors, like blue and red. Tie a big knot in one end and put some tape around it so the beads can't come off. A toothpick taped to one end of the string makes it easier to string on the beads.

Your child strings the beads on, 10 at a time, separating each group of ten with a small piece of blue tape wrapped around the string to keep the groups of 10 separate. Use the red tape after every hundred beads, so that each group of 100 is clearly marked. This continues all the way to 1000, which will probably take multiple bead stringing sessions. That is great, because your child will count the beads on the chain each time to remember how far she has come toward 1000. By this point, your child should be able to count the bead groups by tens and hundreds, saving a lot of time.

This project will produce a great material that perfectly provides concrete, hands-on experience with how many 1000 of something is. Hang the chain on your child's wall. To make printed representations of 1000, lay out 10 printed Hundred Squares from your math printables. Have your child make a stack with these, while counting, "*One hundred, two hundred*"...etc, up to one thousand. Staple these together and write 1000 on the top with a black marker:

To represent 1000 in a more concrete way that provides depth and visual reinforcement, you can get the 10 Wooden Squares of 100 from Montessori Outlet (above) for under $10. Stack the squares to represent 1000. Be sure your child counts all the circles on at least one square to verify that there are 100. The obvious benefit of the stapled hundred square printables is that you can make as many of them as you like for the cost of the paper and ink.

Numbers greater than 1000

Now, continue making amounts and numerals, going from 1000 – 9,999. Make amounts and let your child create the numeral for each amount. Regularly switch it up and make a numeral and have your child create the correct amount:

As your child makes amounts and numerals, always encourage him to state what he is doing. Whether she makes the amount or the numeral in the photos, for example, she says, "*One thousand, three hundred, and seventy four.*"

Work up through 1000-1,999, 2000-2,999, 3,000-3,999, etc., in sequence, making more 1000 stacks and doing many amounts and numerals as you go.

Make sure your child is practicing writing the numerals as he goes. Once you get into numbers greater than 1000, it is also time to learn the place values of the Decimal System.

Decimal System place values

Your child is now making numbers from 1000-1,999. It is fairly simple now to introduce the decimal system place values. First, teach your child the place value names. Set up a layout like this, using the Decimal System Numeral Cards and the Place Value Card from the Math Printables (p.6):

Introduce decimal system place value words. Make a numeral in the 1000's. Point out to your child the words on the Place Value Card: Thousands, Hundreds, Tens, and Units. Read the number with your child: "*One thousand, three hundred, and seventy four.*" Carefully remove the 1000 numeral card and place it over the place value card:

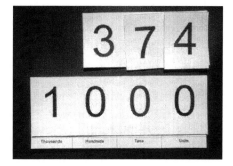

Say, "*Now there is a one in the thousands place, meaning 1000.*" Repeat with the 300 card, moving it down and saying, "*Now there is a 3 in the hundreds place, meaning 300*":

Repeat with the 70 card, saying, "Now there is a 7 in the tens place, meaning 70", and the 4, saying, "Now there is a 4 in the units place, meaning 4." Read the number: "*One thousand, three hundred seventy four.*"

Ask your child to point out what numbers are in the thousands, hundreds, tens, and units places, asking both in and out of order. Do many numerals this way. After a while, you can simply show your child a numeral, like 3,729, and ask what numbers are in which places. Mastering this concept takes practice.

The Montessori Stamp Game

The Montessori Stamp Game is possibly the best material ever invented for teaching children the decimal system. It teaches children the decimal system, and also how to add and subtract larger numbers, including those with remainders.

There are a number of good resources for inexpensively putting together a Stamp Game for home use:

Montessori Print Shop offers a *free* Printable Stamp Game and Instructions set that provides everything your child needs. Open their free materials link and scroll down the page to find these. The instructions alone make this a must-have resource, and you get the whole package free to boot!

Stamp Game by Montessori Tech is a great iPad app.

At: montessorialbum.com, search 'Stamp Game' for tutorials with photos on introducing the Stamp Game and doing all the operations with numbers.

At: montessorimaterials.org/Math/stampgame1.pdf, you will find a free set of Stamp Game printables

At: thelearningark.blogspot.com/2009/04/introducing-stamp-game, you will find a nice pictorial / tutorial on doing the Stamp Game

Search Stamp Game at DiscoveryMoments.com

At the Discovery Moments blog there is a very nice pictorial description of making a DIY Stamp Game using buttons (photo). If you use small round labels to write the 1000, 100, 10, and 1 numerals on the buttons, that would make this version just about perfect.

"Education should no longer be mostly imparting knowledge, but must take a new path, seeking the release of human potentials."

"All our handling of the child will bear fruit, not only at the moment, but in the adult they are destined to become."

Maria Montessori

Operations with Numbers

Hopefully, you came here because you read earlier in the book that your child can be doing these activities at the same time she works through larger amounts and numerals and the Decimal System activities. These activities will expand your child's understanding of math by learning practical things she can do with the amounts and numerals she is working with.

The operations covered here, in order, are addition, multiplication, subtraction, and division. This is a good general order based on the conceptual difficulty of each operation. Children who are ready to do these activities are usually also capable of using digital tablet math apps effectively. These are recommended throughout this and other sections.

Addition

Addition is the easiest operation to learn. While you are working with identical objects during amount activities, it is simple to point out that a group of, say, 3 objects, plus a group of 2 objects, makes, or *equals*, a new group of 5 objects. Use these terms while adding groups together. As your child gets familiar with adding groups together, introduce the + and = signs, by using sign cards, numeral cards, wooden beads or coins, and clear condiment (or similar) cups, as shown below. *"Four plus three equals seven."*

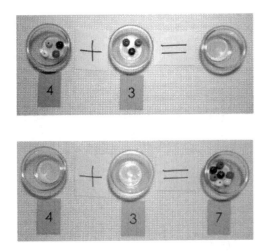

You can also use Unifix Cubes, dice, or beads on a string for doing addition:

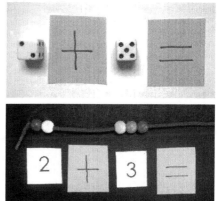

For your first addition problems, stick with sums from 1-10 and avoid problems requiring carrying numbers. Adding larger numbers should also first be done with sums that do not require carrying over to the next decimal place:

Do many problems this way before you introduce one that requires carrying over a ten from the units to the tens place:

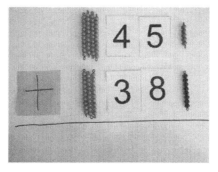

Bring the units bars down, and show your child how to substitute a ten bar for the first ten beads she counts, and the proper remainder, and then carry (literally) the ten bar over to the tens place:

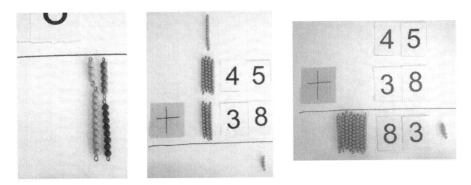

At some point while working with these larger numbers, you can introduce the Montessori Stamp Game (p.66), which combines operations with numbers with learning about the decimal system. The Stamp Game also allows your child to clearly see how to carry numbers from one place to the next and convert amounts, as when $9 + 6 = 15$, which is shown as one ten and five units.

In the Math Printables, you will find Addition Tables. Your child does each problem in turn, using whatever method she prefers, and fills in the answers. By reading the problems and answers top to bottom, your child will start to see the relationships between numbers more clearly. You will also be able to point out that $3+8 = 8+3$, which seems obvious to us but which children need to experience to clearly understand.

Montessori Addition Strip Boards

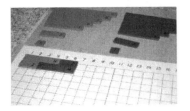

Montessori schools use this simple material to help children see the relationships between numbers when they are added together.

Photo: *The Education of Ours*

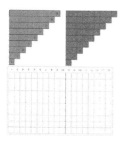

Montessori Print Shop has a very nice printable Addition Strip Board, Charts, + Instructions to download for under $4. This is a perfect material for home use. Print this out onto card stock for added durability.

Montessori Print Shop

Here is a summary of how to use the Addition Strip Boards:

- Write out some simple addition problems using the numbers 1-9.
- Your child finds the blue strip with the first number and sets it on the board horizontally, with the left end lined up with the top left square on the board.
- Your child finds the red strip for the second number, and sets it end to end with the blue strip.
- The sum is on the top of the board, right above the right end of the red strip.

The strip boards are especially good for illustrating the Commutative Law of addition, which states that the order numbers are added in does not affect the final result. The sum is the same, for instance, whether we add 2 + 6 or 6 + 2.

Good iPad apps for doing addition include Montessori Bead Facts Plus Minus, and Adding Apples HD.

For addition tables, check: donnayoung.org/math/addition-charts.htm

Multiplication

Multiplication is a faster form of addition. A few simple activities give your child a nice introduction. The easiest is to have your child count to a certain number a specific number of times. For example, tell your child, "*Let's count to 2, four times.*" Have your child use pennies and set them out as he counts:

"The unknown energy that can help humanity is that which lies hidden in the child."

Maria Montessori

Have your child count the total number of objects – 8. Say, *"Two, times four, is 8"*. Introduce the X sign and write out the problem, or have your child write it out, as: 2 X 4 = 8. Now you can do many multiplication problems this way, writing the final answer down as above for each one.

The Multiplication Board

A multiplication board is another good way to demonstrate and reinforce how multiplication works. You can use the Hundred Board for this, as in the photos, or simply draw a grid of lines on a sheet of card stock and use the numeral cards from the Math Printables.

To do 2 X 4 using the board, tell your child, *"Let's count to two, three times."* Set the 2 above the second square, and count down three on the left and point the arrow at the third square down. Now, help your child as needed to set down pennies in pairs, starting at the top left and counting, *"One, two. One, two. One, two."*. The board will end up like this:

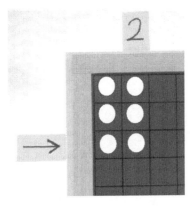

"Two, counted three times, equals six." You can then explain that we say it this way: *"Two times three equals six."* Do many simple multiplication problems this way. Have your child write the problems and answers in the 2 X 3 = 6 format.

Print the Multiplication Tables from your math printables (p.6). Have your child start out with 0 X 0 and progress on through these tables, using the multiplication board, and writing in the answers as she goes. As with the Addition Tables, this makes the relationships between numbers clear. It can also help your child start to learn the multiplication tables, which is practically a lost art in these days of calculators.

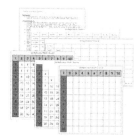

Montessori Print Shop's Multiplication Charts (left) makes a great home activity, and comes with complete instructions. Nice!

Good iPad multiplications apps are Multiplication Charts HD, and Skip Counting.

Subtraction

Introduce subtraction just as you did with addition:

"Seven, minus four, equals three."

Beads on a shoelace also work:

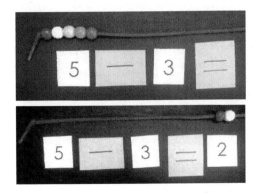

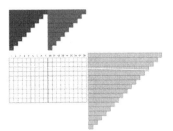

The Subtraction Strip Board, Charts + Instructions (left) from Montessori Print Shop are great printable subtraction materials, for under $4. Good iPad subtraction apps include Subtracting Sardines HD, and Montessori Bead Facts Plus Minus.

Division

For a first division activity, you need a bowl, 3 small cups, and 9 coins:

Tell your child that the three cups belong to three children, and we need to give each child the same number of coins. Have your child count to see that there are 9 coins in the bowl. Let your child think about how she would do this, and try however she likes. If he figures it out, great. If not, show him how to put one coin into each cup, then do this again, and then again, until all the coins are gone from the middle bowl. Have your child count to verify that each cup has 3 coins:

Say, "*Nine divided by 3 equals 3.*" This may not be completely clear right away, as there are better ways to state what your child has just done, such as perhaps, "*Nine divided into three groups leaves 3 in each group.*" Alternate verbal explanations help children fully understand. The goal is to eventually help your child be comfortable with the mathematical statement, "*Nine divided by three equals three.*"

Do many simple division problems this way. Division problems involving carrying tens and using places to the right of the decimal point are generally a bit advanced for this age group. If your child is willing and ready, though, go for it.

The Division Word Problems and the Division Charts from Montessori Print Shop are excellent, inexpensive division materials used in Montessori classrooms all over the world. These materials will extend your child's division activities. The Montessori Division Board iPad app is a great virtual division board.

Solid and Plane Geometric Figures

While your child is working on amounts and numerals, and perhaps has started doing some operations with numbers, she can also start learning about three dimensional and flat, or plane, geometric shapes. We start with the three dimensional shapes because real objects are always the most appropriate starting point with young children. Once these are familiar, we move to flat shapes and figures, helping the child make a gradual move into abstract thought. For the first activities, a set of geometric solids is required. Here are some that work well:

The **Montessori Geometric Solids** with bases, at around $45, is the nicest and priciest material. These are excellent, and can be sold for around $30 when your child is finished with them. Highly recommended.

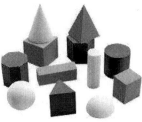

The set of **19 Geometric Solids from Learning Resources** are nice wooden shapes for under $30. Put them in a nice basket with a colorful cloth for your child's shelves.

The **Didax Easyshapes 3D Geometric Shapes** are made of foam and make a nice set for learning shapes. Around $16.

The **Montessori Mystery Bags with Geometric Shapes** (p.25) are another good alternative, and come with two nice bags for stereognostic sense activities.

Naming the shapes

In your math printables (p.6) there is a set of Geometric Shape Names. Print these out and use them to teach your child the names of all the shapes. You can do Three Step Lessons, or simply lay the solids out and match their names to them. It always helps your child remember if she feels a shape while also looking at it and saying its name. If your child is not learning to read yet, recognizing the names will take a while, but it is important to introduce them.

While doing these activities, allow your child plenty of time to simply handle the shapes. That is when much of the valuable learning occurs.

Flat and curved

Show your child what straight and curved mean and let her sort the solids into groups tagged with name cards that say 'flat', 'curved', and 'flat + curved'. The cylinder and cone have a combination of flat and curved sides. You can also point out that the curved sided solids roll, while the straight sided shapes do not. The straight sided forms can be stacked, while the curved forms cannot, at least on their curved sides.

How many sides?

Encourage your child to compare the shapes by counting how many sides, or faces, each one has. How many sides does a sphere have?

Matching shapes to their bases

The Montessori shapes come with a set of bases for the shapes to sit on. If you get a different set, trace all the aspects of the shapes onto card stock and cut these shapes out to serve as square, rectangular, and circular bases. Set them out and have your child predict which shapes can fit which ways onto which bases.

The Mystery Bag

If you get the Mystery Bag with Geometric Shapes (p.25), you are all set for this activity. If you get a different set of shapes, just use a suitable bag, or even a big sock, for a mystery bag. Once your child learns the names of the shapes, place them one at a time in the bag and let your child identify them by feel. This develops the stereognostic sense – the ability to identify objects by feel. Find objects around your home that have geometric shapes, like cylinders, spice or other jars, square and rectangular boxes, balls, etc. Use these in the mystery bag and have your child tell you which shape each object is.

Another great sensorial activity is to place different objects, like a feather, a rubber band, a smooth glass object, fabrics of different kinds and feel, small stuffed animals, a sponge, etc., in the mystery bag one at a time and have your child describe each object before naming it. Help as needed to give your child new language like *soft, firm, elastic, compressible, rough, smooth, slick, spongy, sharp, pointed, edges, rubbery*, etc.

Making shapes

At: fun-stuff-to-do.com/geometric-shapes-to-print, you will find free pdf printables for geometric shapes patterns. Print and cut these out and fold them to make the shapes. This is a wonderful geometry and small muscle exercise activity. It may take a few tries to make shapes, but stick with it. Many more complicated shape printables are available at: korthalsaltes.com

Search shapes online

Search each shape name online and check out the images and video links. You will find all kinds of examples of shapes and interesting things they make.

When your child has worked with three dimensional shapes for a while, introduce flat, or plane shapes. In the math printables there are printouts for the basic shapes and their names. Here are more good resources:

From Montessori Print Shop: Geometric Solid Sorting Cards (left), Geometric Solid Three Part Cards (middle), and Geometric Solids Worksheets (right).

Plane figures

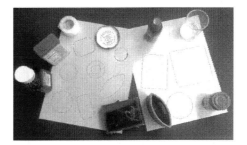

A nice start with plane figures is to trace objects from around your home (above). Jars, boxes, knick knacks, many things will work. Puzzles like the Melissa & Doug Shapes Chunky Puzzle introduce basic flat shapes, but with a bit of thickness to help younger children transition to images on paper:

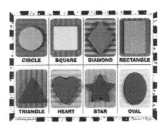

Tracing these shapes is a great activity. Next, print out the geometric shapes from the math printables. The shapes are: square, rectangle, pentagon, hexagon, circle, oval, trapezoid, right triangle, triangle, and parallelogram. Print out the shape names and work with your child to match them up:

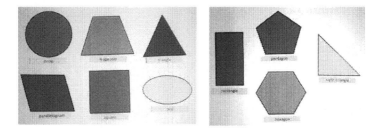

To make your own set of thicker, more durable shapes using the above as templates, follow these steps:

- Gather colorful paper, paper spray mounting glue, 14 point illustration board (office supply or crafts store) or a science project display board (walmart), a pair of shears or heavy duty scissors, a pack of glue on wood knobs (crafts store), and a sheet of 400 grit wet / dry sandpaper (hardware store).

- Print out the shapes onto the paper, but don't cut them out yet.

- Glue the full paper sheets onto the board using the spray glue.

- Carefully cut out each shape.

- Lightly sand the edges of the shapes with the sandpaper.

- Glue on a knob in the center of each shape.

- Place the shapes in a little tray:

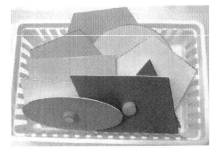

The Learning Resources Primary Shapes Template Set (below, around $7) provides experience with basic shapes and valuable tracing practice, which is a great preparation for writing letters and numerals:

The Didax Montessori Shapes (above, around $35) copy the more expensive metal insets used in Montessori schools, and work well for home use. They provide experiences with positive and negative space, basic shapes, and valuable tracing practice using the outside of the center shapes or the inside of the empty shapes. Your child can overlay shapes to make all kinds of designs.

Geo Boards are another great way to introduce and explore with shapes:

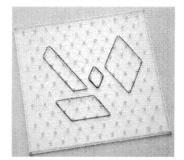

Possibly the best type of geo board for preschoolers are the plastic boards pictured above that have protrusions sticking up to stretch colored rubber bands around to make different shapes. The nails or pushpins commonly used in homemade geo boards can come loose and present a safety hazard. Learning Resources is a good online source for geo boards.

Let your child freely explore making all kinds of shapes. Putting the rubber bands on and stretching them around the pegs is good small muscle exercise. Next, show your child basic shapes printed on cards and let her try to match them on the geo board with rubber bands. Counting the pegs on squares and rectangles will give your child concrete experience in how certain shapes have equal and unequal sides. Virtual, online geo boards can be found at:

mathlearningcenter.org/web-apps/geoboard

mathplayground.com/geoboard

iPad apps for geo board work include the free Geoboard, and Mosaic HD.

Montessori Blue Constructive Triangles

You will find a set of Montessori Blue Constructive Triangles in every Montessori preschool. At under $15, this is an affordable and highly recommended material for home use. I will also show you how to make a set for a bit less money from crafts foam.

Safety Note: These triangles, like all Montessori dimensional materials, are precisely made and have sharp points. Be sure your child always handles them carefully.

The set consists of 12 blue, right angled, scalene triangles that can be combined in many ways to make other shapes. Exploring with making shapes is the essence of this material. To make a cheaper set of triangles, print out the triangles from the Math Printables (p.6) onto colored card stock. A nice pdf file of blue triangle master shapes can be downloaded by searching 'blue triangles' at: thehelpfulgarden.blogspot.com.

Montessori Print Shop has a beautiful Constructive Triangles Blue Design Box printable for $0.99. For a bit thicker set of triangles, use your card stock triangles to trace and cut out another set from crafts foam sheets, which can be found at all crafts stores and Walmart. At Montessori For Everyone, download and print the Triangle Stars pdf for activity ideas. Many other activity ideas can be found by searching 'Montessori blue triangle activities' online.

Start by allowing your child to freely explore combining triangles to make different shapes. Show your child these basic shapes, and make name cards for them, or use the name cards from the math printables:

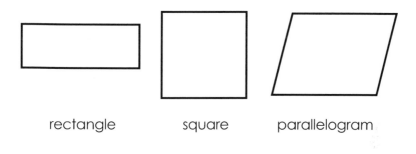

rectangle   square   parallelogram

Here are more triangles your child can make:

Photo: Montessori Outlet

Clockwise from top left: kite, equilateral triangle (all sides the same length), parallelogram, rectangle, parallelogram, isosceles obtuse triangle. Next, explore making various patterns, like these:

For even more fun with triangles, get the Constructive Triangles – Small Hexagonal Box printable for only $0.99 from Montessori Print Shop.

Fractions

The concept of dividing one thing into smaller parts can be challenging for a preschooler. To help your child be ready, make sure he has done lots of work with amounts and numerals up to at least 100, simple operations with numbers, and geometric shapes first. Like most math concepts, when the time is right, introducing your child to fractions can be done pretty easily.

Print out the Fractions Sheets from your Math Printables (p.6). In keeping with the pattern of using real objects first, start with food items. Fruits work perfectly:

Show your child one banana. Cut it in two halves and tell your child that each piece is one half. Continue with quarters. Do the same with an apple, then a little individual serving block of cheese. You can do the same activity with a flat sheet of playdoh cut into a square with a box lid:

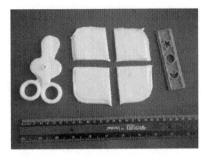

Another fun fractions project uses colored paper plates. This provides a visual representation of fractions as they relate to a whole. You'll need at least two colors of paper plates of the same size, a ruler, a marker, and a pair of scissors.

Measure halves and quarters and cut colored plates to show ½ and ¼. You can obviously do 1/3, also. Set these on white plates to clearly show these fractional divisions, as in the photo above. You can also draw lines on the white plates using the colored plates as guides, and write in the numerals for the fractions:

Your child can also put sections of the paper plates, marked with their fraction numerals, together to remake whole plates:

Next, print out the <u>Fractions sheets</u> from your math printables (p.6) and start using these for more fractions activities. Montessori Print Shop has a nice set of

Fraction Cards and Labels that includes 31 three part fractions cards, labels, and black line masters, for around $3:

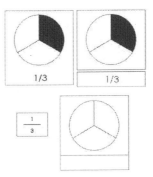

There are a number of nice, free fractions printables at Montessorimaterials.org (montessorimaterials.org/math1.html).

Math-Aids.com has fractions worksheets, choose the pie wedge and rectangular bar options (math-aids.com/fractions/fractions_lesson_plan.html).

Good iPad apps for learning fractions include Pizza Fractions 1, Tap to Learn's Fractions App, and Match the Fraction. A good android app is Fraction Circle.

With any of these resources available, you can easily introduce your child to ½, ¼, and 1/3, including the numerals. After this, work up through 1/5, 1/6, 1/7, etc.

"The essential thing is to arouse such an interest that it engages the child's whole personality."

"No adult can bear a child's burden or grow up in his stead."

"The hands are the instruments of man's intelligence."

Maria Montessori

Using Math Every Day

Now you can start showing your child ways to use her new math skills in daily life. This reinforces all the activities your child has been doing. Learning these skills increases a child's sense of independence and self-confidence. The sooner a young child sees herself as a competent person who is able to function well in daily life, the better.

Do these activities whenever your child is interested, for as long as he wants to. If he loses focus, try to refocus him, but when he wants to move to something else, let him. Children develop the ability to focus their attention and concentration gradually, by using fun materials that naturally draw their interest.

Whenever possible, make activities self-contained in a box or bowl for your child's shelves. This allows for independent use and exploration, which helps a child catch those moments when she is able to focus on an activity and make the most of them.

Inches & Feet

Get your child her own ruler and simple tape measure. Show your child the inch markers (or the centimeters if you are using the metric system) and count them. Tell her that twelve inches equals one foot. Show her how each foot is clearly marked on the tape measure. Now he can measure all kinds of things:

Measure your child's height using the tape measure and making a mark on the wall or doorway. Help him as needed to stretch out the tape measure and read how tall he is. Write it down in feet and inches. Measure everyone in your family and make a sheet with everyone's height on it. Repeat regularly to chart your child's growth.

Show your child how to measure a TV screen from corner to corner diagonally. The next time you go to a store, take the tape measure and check a few TV's to see if their screens are their listed sizes.

Set different objects on a table and make a game of estimating how tall or wide each one is in inches. You can use cups and glasses, little boxes, balls, figurines, knick knacks, index cards, books, photos, etc. Take turns guessing how high each one is and then measuring it with the ruler. Your child's ability to estimate will gradually improve.

Team up with your child to measure and cut straws into lengths from 1" to 10" in one inch increments. Make a graded row from shortest to longest. She can do this with playdoh 'snakes' also:

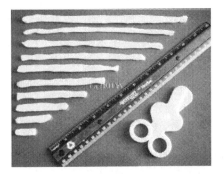

Help your child as needed to roll long snakes. Show him how to measure and cut snakes to 1", 2", 3', etc. lengths up to 10", making ten snakes. Lay them carefully in a graded sequence as in the photo. You can each measure and cut some of the snakes and check each other's work.

"The task of the educator lies in seeing that the child does not confound good with immobility and evil with activity."

Maria Montessori

Treasure Hunt

Combine experiences in using a compass and a tape measure with this fun geography and math activity for 5-7 year olds. Every child should have an inexpensive compass. If you don't already have a tape measure, get one like the one shown. Review using each tool with your child:

Using a globe (your child does have a globe, right?) and Google Earth, show you child where North, South, East, and West are in relation to where she is standing on the Earth. Now, take the compass to your yard and find each direction. Verifying them on a paper map helps.

Your child may have worked with a ruler or tape measure earlier and be familiar with the inches and feet markings. If not, do the measuring activities shown just before this.

Hide coins or some other cool treasure in your yard, out of sight under something. Starting at your back door or wherever your child will start, measure out a course leading to the treasure. Go a certain number of feet in one direction, then another, keeping track of each distance and change in direction by drawing up a map. Your course ends at the treasure.

Now you will have a map with printed and drawn directions like, *"Start at the back door. Go 10 feet straight west, then 12 feet north. Now, go west 6 feet, then east 15 feet. Go south 12 feet to the treasure."*

Your child follows the map, measuring out the distances and following the directions using the compass. Help as needed, such as by holding one end of the tape measure. Your child can place stakes with a hammer at turning points if desired. When your child reaches the end, she will find the treasure.

Extend the activity by making the compass - along with the binoculars and magnifying glass - a regular companion on your nature trips. Just getting out in nature is one of the best learning experiences for young children. Make regular family trips to parks, forests, lakes, and other natural areas a habit. Everyone will benefit!

Estimating Pennies

Here's a fun one! Use little dabs of playdoh to stand a quarter, penny, and nickel on end, as in the photo. Lay 5-6 pennies out on the table. Ask your child how many pennies she thinks she will need to stack to make a stack as high as the quarter. Try her estimate out.

It will take 12 pennies, which is probably more than your child guessed. This is probably partly because you only had 5-6 pennies laid out, so your child may assume that is all she has to work with. This adds a 'thinking outside the box' element to the activity. Repeat with the penny and nickel. This is a great exercise in estimation and critical thinking.

My Amazing Hands

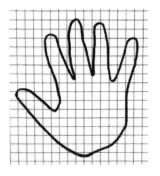

This activity for 5-7 year olds includes different ways your child can measure using her hands, to introduce different types of measurement with one activity. You will need:

- A sheet of graph paper for each hand you want to measure
- Two nesting bowls
- Dry beans in a bowl (like kidney, pinto, or lima)
- Measuring cup with an 'ml' (milliliter) scale
- Tape measure or ruler
- Water
- Blank sheet of paper and pencil

Make lines to divide the sheet of blank paper into 4 equal sections. Label these:

Length: how long is my hand?

Surface Area: how big is my hand?

Capacity: how much does my hand hold?

Volume: how much water does my hand move?

These measurements are stated in simple form first. When you write the results down you can introduce the formal terms length, surface area, capacity, and volume. Write these at the bottom of each square on the sheet.

To measure length, have your child spread his hand out on the table. Measure the length from the farthest point on the wrist to the end of the longest finger. Record it on the chart in the section labeled, *"How long is my hand?"*

To measure the surface area, have your child spread his hand out on the graph paper. Trace his hand. Count all the squares inside the hand tracing. Count even partially covered squares as 1 square for simplicity. Record the result on the chart in number of squares under: *How big is my hand?"*

To measure capacity, have your child pick up as many beans as he can hold without dropping any and drop them into an empty bowl. Now he counts how many beans he picked up. Record the result under the section labeled, *"How much does my hand hold?"*

To measure volume, fill up the smaller of the two nesting bowls with water right to the rim. Set it inside the larger bowl. Have your child make a fist and slowly lower it up to the wrist into the water. Watch the water spill over into the larger bowl. Remove the smaller bowl carefully. Now, pour the water from the larger bowl into the measuring cup. Record the result in the section labeled, *"How much water does my hand move?"*

Try this activity with other family member's hands and record and compare the results on a chart for the wall.

Baric Touch

This is a fun math and sensory activity for 4-7 year olds. Baric means weight. In this activity, your child learns to match cups of the same weight by feeling them; and to recognize progressively smaller differences in the weight of the cups. You will need:

- Quarters and pennies
- Blindfold (easiest: tape over the eye holes of a costume mask)
- Marker
- Clear, identical cups, like Diamond Multipurpose Mini-Cups

Set out 8 cups in 4 pairs. Have your child count out 1 quarter each into two cups, 3 quarters each into the next two cups, 6 quarters each into the next two cups, and 10 quarters each into the last pair of cups. Help her if needed to write the numerals on each cup showing how many quarters are in each cup (photo).

Have your child put on the blindfold and hold out his hands, palms up. Place a cup with 1 quarter in one of his hands and ask him to bounce it slightly up and down to feel the weight. Place a cup with 6 or 10 quarters in the other hand and ask him to compare them and tell you if they feel the *same* or *different*. He should say that they feel different. Let him lift the blindfold and see that the cups have different amounts of quarters.

Repeat this until your child has matched all 4 pairs of cups by weight. When your child is ready, change the number of quarters in the cups to make them closer in weight. You might try cups with 1, 3, 5, and 7 quarters, for example, to make it more challenging. Be sure to put the blindfold on yourself and have your child give you cups to compare and match by weight.

With practice, you may be able to feel the difference of just a single quarter.

Scales

Scales provide excellent math experiences. A 4 oz. mechanical postal scale is great because it has a visible bar that used to read the weight. This is a much better visual and real world experience for a young child than a digital scale. The little flat tray can hold a wide variety of objects and little containers for weighing different objects.

A bathroom scale with a dial also works very well. This kind of scale again provides direct visual feedback as the hand moves around the dial when weight is applied. There are also great scales especially designed for children.

The Baby Bear Scale from Discount School Supply has plastic bears to weigh. You can use many other items like coins, paper clips, cotton balls, etc. Another excellent child's scale is the Learning Resources Primary Bucket Balance, which can also hold and measure liquids.

Activities with scales

- Balance the scales by counting identical numbers of identical objects into the containers, such as coins, paper clips, counting bears, etc.

- When you go the store, take the time to weigh your fruits and veggies using the scales. This is a great experience in math and measurement. Take one fruit out and see what happens. Do calculations on the fly. Make this a regular feature of your shopping trips.

- See how many pennies it takes to balance with a certain number of quarters.

- Balance the containers with objects, then weigh the objects on a postal scale to verify that the two groups weight the same.

- Use two additional containers to hold objects inside the scale's containers, and introduce the practice of weighing the containers first.

- Do addition and subtraction problems using objects on the scales.

- Push down on the postal scale with eyes closed and try to make it read 1oz, 2oz, etc.

- Try balancing heavier objects, like coins, with very light objects, like cotton balls. This introduces new concepts of mass and weight. See how many cotton balls it takes on one side only to make that side drop down.

- Measure 1 oz. or ¼ cup of fluid, or teaspoons / tablespoons of rice or other material into each container with a measuring cup or plastic medicine cup and see if they balance. Use an eyedropper to add one drop at a time to one container to see how many drops it takes to cause the scales to be out of balance.

- Get a set of hexagram weights (search on Amazon) and do addition and subtraction problems with them, writing the problems out and completing them on the scale.

- Using the bathroom scale with dial, weigh smaller, heavier objects and compare this with lighter, large objects like empty cardboard boxes, styrofoam flower blocks, etc. This further introduces concepts of weight, size, and mass.

Good measurement tablet apps include My First Weighing Exercises (android), Kids Measurement Science (android), and Kids Math – Measurement Worksheets (iPad).

Search 'measure' on kidsactivitiesblog.com, and 'foot fun' on education.com for more activity ideas.

Egg Carton Math

 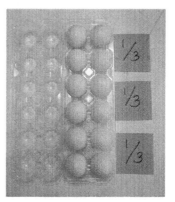

An egg carton and a dozen plastic easter eggs, plastic practice golf balls, or ping pong balls can be used for a number of great math activities:

- Have your child count out 12 as he places an object in each depression.
- Count by two's and place numeral post-it note labels as at left above.
- Divide the 12 balls into two equal groups and demonstrate fractions by placing six at a time in the carton and labeling each group as ½. Repeat by making three equal groups and labeling each as 1/3, as at right above.
- Place different numbers of balls in the carton, have your child put on a blindfold, and let him count them by feel.
- Help your child as needed to draw graphic representations using circles of the various groups possible.

Other containers with depressions, like muffin tins and chocolate candy trays, can be used for counting and demonstrating 1:1 correspondence.

Cardinal, Ordinal, and Nominal Numbers

You have mostly been working with cardinal numbers with your child. Cardinal numbers represent how many there are of something. This is the most common type of number. An ordinal number denotes the position of something in a list or line. It tells you what place something occupies in an ordered group, like a line of playdoh balls or marbles on golf tees:

When your child works with activities like these, take a minute and start at the left end of a line of objects. Count them left to right in a new way: "*First, second, third, fourth, fifth*", etc. Go only up to the tenth at first. Give your child practice counting this way with different lineups of objects. Ask her to point out the third, sixth, first, etc. Move the objects into new positions in the lineup and repeat, so that your child sees that changing position changes the ordinal number.

Nominal numbers are used like names for things. Examples are the number on the jersey of a person playing sports, or on a race car. Search online for images of these for examples. Here is an example, from Best Coloring Pages for Kids:

In the image above, there are 3 cars (Cardinal number). Car number 21 (Nominal number) is in first place (Ordinal number. Help your child as needed to continue identifying the cars by their number types.

Counting Cars & People

A friend of mine started a company called Countermeasures, whose sole service was counting cars that pulled into parking lots or used highway exits and entrances. You can do the same thing as a math activity with your child. When you are at the store or in a waiting room, count the cars and people. You can watch a particular entrance and count cars and people as they move through it. Make a contest out of guessing. Count the number of cars that are silver, red, black, etc. Estimate how many cars are in one section of a parking lot, and then count to check your estimates and see who came the closest. There are all kinds of number games you can play.

Telling Time

Shutterstock

Learning to tell time, like all practical life skills leading toward independence, is a big deal for a young child. As with basic math, it is easy to move too quickly, before a foundation of understanding is developed.

Children have a much different experience of time than adults. It is important to first give your child experiences with the common units of time passing. Seconds, minutes, and hours are arbitrary periods of time that a child becomes familiar with by experiencing them directly. Once this is done, we can associate those units of time with the numbers and marks on the clock.

When she can tell time, your child can be responsible for getting things done and being ready to go on time. He can keep track of when to call home and when a favorite TV show is on. Telling time is a big accomplishment!

A battery operated, analog clock with a white face, black numerals, 60 marks for seconds & minutes, the hour numbers, and the three hands – seconds, minutes, and hours, is a great first clock for a child. Most office supply stores have these. They everything needed to clearly tell time, without distracting visual elements.

Seconds

Show your child the clock. Point out the 60 marks around the edge. Tell your child, *"These marks stand for both seconds and minutes. First, we'll do seconds. One second is a very short time."* Point out the second hand. When it reaches the top, start counting 1, 2, 3….as it ticks each second. Count along with your child and the second hand to 60 seconds. Clapping every second helps make it clear how long as second is and demonstrates the consistent flow of time.

Pick a time the second hand reaches the top again and let your child count the seconds by herself. Ask your child, *"How many second marks are there between the numbers?"* Help your child if needed to determine that there are 5. Clap off the seconds between two larger lines.

Ask your child, *"What can we do in one second?"* Try clapping hands, jumping up and down once, Standing up and sitting down, etc. This gives your child real time experience in how long one second is. Try this for 5, then 10, then 15 etc. seconds so your child gets a real idea of those time periods. See how many seconds each of you can stand on one foot, or how many seconds it takes to run around the living room. *"*

Minutes

Now, let's do minutes. A minute is a longer than a second. 60 Seconds make 1 minute. When the second hand goes all the way around the circle, that is one minute. Do you think we can sit absolutely still for one minute?"

Watch quietly with your child and try not to move as you watch the second hand make a complete revolution. Did you both make it? Try washing your hands, walking around the house, checking the mail, getting a drink of water, etc. See what you can do in one minute. Estimating and testing will help your child learn how long one minute is.

Note where the minute hand is and watch the second hand go all the way around. Count the seconds as they pass. *"The 60 marks also stand for minutes. One circle around for the second hand is 60 seconds. For the Minute Hand – point to the minute hand – that is just one minute."* Do this again to emphasize how the minute hand only moves one mark every time the second hand goes around 60 marks.

Hours

When the <u>minute</u> hand (point to the minute hand) goes all the way around the circle, that makes 1 hour. 60 minutes make 1 hour." Show your child the hour hand. Point out to your child that the written numbers on the clock stand for hours. Count to show there are 12 hours. Ask your child what she thinks you two can do in one hour. Could you go to the store, watch a long TV show, watch a movie, take a bath? Get your child's ideas. Estimate and test.

When the clock hits any hour exactly, tell your child, *"We're going to see how long an hour is."* Set the alarm on that clock or another one to go off in one hour. Find an errand to run, a TV show you can watch, something that might take an hour. Note clearly with your child what number the small hand is pointing to. If, for example, it points to the 3, tell your child, *"When the small hand points to the 4 it will have been one hour."* Do your thing together, and take a look at the clock afterwards to see if the small hand has made it to the 4. If not, keep checking on it until it has been an hour. If you went over, discuss how your activity took more than one hour.

Now that your child has experienced units of time, she can learn to identify time on the clock and read and write what time it is. Tablet apps can be very useful here. Good iPad apps for telling time include Telling Time HD, Telling Time Free, and Telling Time the Easy Way. Good android time telling apps include Clock Time for Kids and Interactive Telling Time HD.

The Learning Resources Big Time Student Clock, for under $10, is an excellent teaching tool that eliminates any distracting elements.

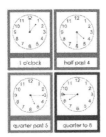

The Clock Series printables from Montessori Print Shop are great teaching aids, used in Montessori schools all over the world.

Start by showing your child how the hands look at one o'clock, two o'clock, three o'clock, etc. Use printables to give your child practice identifying time on the hour. Use your child's wall clock or the Learning Resources clock and move the hands to various positions on the hour for your child to identify.

Find free printable worksheets at: homeschoolmath.net/worksheets/clock.php

More great time printables can be found at: enchantedlearning.com/time

Donna Young has clock printables at: donnayoung.org/math/clock.htm

Next, have your child place the hands at one o'clock. Show your child the minute hand, and ask her to move it to 5 minutes after one o'clock. Help her as needed to move the hand slowly and count off the minute marks. Repeat, starting at different hour points (two o'clock, seven o'clock, etc).

Do the above activity at 10 minutes, and then 15 minutes, after the hour. You can point out that 15 minutes is called a quarter hour. If your child is doing fractions, you can use a printed clock face to show how the clock can be divided into four quarters with the lines falling at the 15 minute multiples: 15, 30, 45, 60. This can also be an addition activity: start with 15 and add 15 each time, up to 60. Quarter hour printables can be found at: yescoloring.com/tell-time.html

Continue this way, printing out more worksheets and doing 30 and 45 minutes after the hour, so that your child becomes really familiar with recognizing and naming these times. Work in the digital numerals (4:45, 6:30, etc) as you work on these times. The clock dominoes game (link given previously) is great for this.

Next, work on calling time from 1-30 minutes *after* the last hour, and time from 30-1 minute *before* the next hour; and learning about am and pm. Finally, introduce calling the individual minutes between the quarter and half hour times. This is when a digital clock really shines, as it clearly shows each minute as it passes.

When your child starts telling time, let her watch your clocks when it is time to do things on your schedule. Let your child help reset the clocks for daylight savings time. Check your home clocks against the standard US time at: http://time.gov/HTML5/. This helps your child see the practical uses of telling time.

Using a Calendar

One of the best ways for a young child to learn about the calendar is to simply put up a planning calendar on the wall in her room and use it every day. Make sure that the days of the week and the numbers are clearly displayed. As with the clock, a calendar that simply shows the month, days of the week, and numbers of the days, along with an image of the previous and next months, is better than one having a lot of visual distractions.

Each day, have your child make a mark or other sign on the days date. Say the day and month every day – *"Today is the 15th of June, 2011."* You can add in weather information and talk about the plan for the day. Your child will start to see the progression of days, weeks, and months. Write in major holidays, family birthdays, and other important dates. Any time your child shows interest, help him memorize the days of the week. Point to them and practice reading them. Let him practice writing them. Count through the entire calendar to find out how many weeks there are in one year.

You can also introduce the 12 months of the year and practice recognizing and writing them. Most calendars have a page with all the months of the year that is good for this. It is always a good activity to point out to your child how some months have 30 days, others 31, and to learn the old rhyme: *"Thirty days has September, April, June, and November. All the rest have 31 except February, with 28 days clear, and 29 every four years on leap year."*

Once your child has used a calendar regularly through a couple of years she will have it down for life. There are a thousand calendar activities. Few are more effective than actually using one.

Get free printable calendars at: freeprintable.com/free-printable-calendars

Money

You have probably done some of the activities using coins and a dollar, such as sorting, coin exchanges, and making amounts greater than 10 using coins while doing amounts and numerals earlier. Now, you can extend your child's money experiences into buying, selling, making change, saving, and shopping.

Splash Money is an excellent iPad app for teaching children about money. Also, check out the Kids and Money series at the Carrots Are Orange blog.

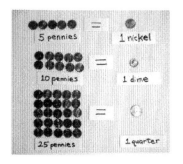

You may already have done the activity shown at left. Get out 25 pennies, a nickel, a dime, and a quarter. Show your child that 5 pennies make one nickel, 10 pennies make one dime (you did this one earlier), and 25 pennies make one quarter. Lay out the coins and = sign cards to give your child a visual experience of these coin amounts.

Give your child 5, then 10, then 25 pennies and let her figure out to give you first a nickel, then a dime, and finally a quarter back. Then do it in reverse – give you child a nickel, dime and then a quarter and have your child give you the correct number of pennies back. Work on this until you feel your child understands these coins and the amounts they represent. Now try it with two nickels, then two dimes, then two quarters. Use the Hundred Board if needed to help your child figure things out. Keep playing this game, adding more nickels, dimes, and quarters as your child gets more comfortable.

Making a dollar

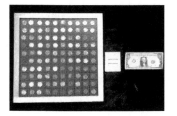

Children love to start using bills! First, explain that a dollar is 100 pennies. Then use the Hundred Board to lay it out. You can also just draw a grid of 100 squares on a piece of paper. Place an = sign and then a dollar to the right of the board with 100 pennies and read with your child, "*1oo pennies equals one dollar*."

Ask your child, *"Do you want to find out how many nickels, dimes, and quarters make a dollar?"* If the answer is yes, here you go: Have your child set out a floor rug or table mat. *"There are 10 pennies in one dime. How many dimes do you think it takes to make a dollar?"* "*Let's find out!*"

Have your child count the first row of pennies, left to right, removing the pennies as she goes. When she gets to the end, have her place a dime on the last square in the row. Repeat for the other rows. When your child is done, have him count the dimes. *"Ten dimes make one dollar."*

Now repeat these steps with nickels and quarters. Your child starts counting squares at the top left square and puts a nickel down every five squares. Have your child count the nickels. *"Twenty nickels makes one dollar."* Your child repeats the above, but counting to twenty five four times, and putting a quarter down every time she reaches twenty five. *"Four quarters make one dollar."*

Buy & sell

Now your child can 'buy and sell'. Collect groups of objects to sell to each other. Each of you gets an amount of real money, like 5 one dollar bills and a collection of coins.

A toy cash register like the Learning Resources Pretend and Play in the photo can make this really fun and introduce new experiences, such as the practical life skill of buying at a store. Start with even dollars, then introduce how the decimal point is used with amounts like $1.10, $2.25, $1.05. As your child gets better, she can count by 10's, 5's, and 25's. Help as needed and encourage counting to verify amounts. Refer back to the Hundred Board and decimal system activities as needed to demonstrate. Sell items back for a higher price to teach the concept of making a profit.

App Toy – Cash Register is a fun iPad app. At: countingcoconuts.blogspot.com, search 'money matters' for great activities. Nice play money printables can be found at: donnayoung.org/math/play-money.htm

Money Exchange Game

At The Education of Ours (educationofours.blogspot.com), search 'money exchange game' for a great money game. Each player takes turns rolling dice and collecting the amount shown on the dice (which also involves addition). Whenever these coins can be exchanged for higher value coins, they are. The game ends when each player has one dollar in coins. Here is how you play:

Set out one bowl each of quarters, dimes, nickels, and pennies, along with a one dollar bill for each player. A pair of dice is the only other material. Each player rolls the dice in turn, adding the total dots on the two dice and taking that much in coins. Here is how the players take coins from the bowls:

- **For rolls of 2 – 4, take 2 – 4 pennies**
- **For rolls of 5, take 1 nickel**
- **For rolls of 6 – 9, take 1 nickel and the correct number of pennies**
- **For rolls of 10 (double 5's), take 1 dime**
- **For rolls of 11 – 12, take 1 dime and the correct number of pennies**

Coin exchanges are made as follows:

- **When a player has more than 5 pennies, they are exchanged for 1 nickel**
- **When a player has more than 2 nickels, they are exchanged for 1 dime**
- **When a player has enough dimes and nickels, they are exchanged for quarters**

When a player reaches one dollar in coins, they exchange them for a dollar bill. You can play so that this person is the winner, or until all have reached one dollar to make it more cooperative. Play this game anywhere!

Find coin exchange quizzes at: donnayoung.org/math/money-quiz.htm

Saving

A child's coin bank and a regular small allowance are great first experiences for young children in managing money. Your child can keep a written record of how much money goes into the bank, then total it up and check it for accuracy when the bank is emptied. Saving up for something is another good experience, as is

starting a bank account and making regular deposits. Your child should go with you to the bank, keep the deposit receipts in an envelope, and keep a passbook record of his savings. It is generally not recommended to pay children for doing chores. Children need to learn that everyone in a family makes a contribution of their time and effort to keep the home clean, the shelves stocked, and the family going. Most families are not profit generating enterprises, so there is no need to pay children as if they were employees. A small, regular allowance does give a child experiences in saving, spending, and tracking.

Cashing In

A set of coin tubes make it easy to organize coins to cash in at the bank. Let your child do it independently as much as possible. Keep a running total and go to the bank together to cash them in. Does the bank's total agree with yours?

Some stores have automatic machines for pouring coins in while the machine keeps a running total. Estimate how much you have in coins before you go and write it down. Let your child drop the coins into the hopper and keep an eye on the growing total. Cashing them in is an exercise in exchanging money.

Money Games

Monopoly Junior is a wonderful game when your child is old enough. It involves counting dice and money, buying and selling, collecting rents, and the concept of owning property.

PayDay is a classic game that teaches about earning money and paying bills.

Money Bags teaches coin combining and counting skills while having fun.

Moneywise Kids is a fun board game for counting and exchanging money.

There is a free money counting game at: apples4theteacher.com

At: familylearning.org You will find a collection of good free money games

Fun money games can be found at: kidsmathgamesonline.com/money.html

Shopping

Shopping is one of the best money experiences, even for very young children. As soon as a child can count, she can start understanding how we buy things and begin to learn the value of money. Research shows that an early introduction to money results in increased financial responsibility as the child gets older.

Young children are most concerned with what directly affects them, so start with something your child wants. You can branch out into other shopping experiences later. Here are ideas:

- Do not buy routinely buy your child something every time you go to a store. Prepare your child beforehand by saying something like, "*We are here to buy a gift for _____, not things for ourselves.*" Never buy your child something to get her to stop begging or throwing a fit about it. Giving in and buying something will only reinforce these behaviors.

- Rather than let your child beg for things as you go through a store, give your child a fixed amount of money to buy what he wants. He can decide between a snack and a toy, for example, by comparing the prices and choosing which she wants more.

- Encourage your child to set a goal of buying something he wants, and save up for it. Help him as needed to keep track of his progress.

- Set up three jars or piggy banks, marked 'Saving', 'Spending', and 'Sharing'. The Sharing container is for gifts or to donate to a worthy cause. Choosing a cause, such as protecting animals or helping the poor, and making regular donations, is a wonderful experience for a child. Take the Spend container to the store and limit purchases to the amount inside.

- Involve your child in clipping and printing out coupons. At the store, let your child help identify these products.

- It doesn't directly involve money, but while shopping, teach your child courtesy and manners. Learning to move to allow others to pass, say 'Excuse me', and wait patiently in line are great experiences.

- Do your own quality comparisons. Buy a cheaper (generic) and the more expensive brand name version of items such as paper towels, pasta, and soups. Try them out and discuss if the more expensive brand was worth it and why.

- Let your child help total up the cost of items ordered online.

Money goals by age 6

By age 6, aim for your child to have achieved these goals involving money:

Identifying money

Making change

Being responsible for handling money safely (don't replace money lost)

Learning to save money

Understanding that things cost money

Be able to save for desired purchases

Participate constructively in shopping

Handling an allowance

Estimation

Estimating is an important math and perceptual skill. Work on it regularly with activities appropriate to your child's current level of understanding as you move through the math sequence. Here are ideas:

- When you purchase things that come as a bunch in a bag, play a game of estimating how many are in the bag. Write down your estimates and count the items. Who came the closest? Repackage the items in another container.

- Estimate distances. Start by getting familiar with one foot. Estimate how many feet it is across the room, your yard, etc. Write your estimates down and then measure with the tape measure. Estimate how long it will take to drive to your destination.

- Find a small rectangular container around 5-6" long. Get a few straws. Leave one straw full length, and cut the others to various lengths. Make about half that will fit lengthwise in the container, and half that are too long. Show your child how a straw can fit laid lengthwise in the box. Ask your child to make two groups of straws by estimating which will fit laying in the box and which are too long.

- Gather a few different size small containers, bowls, boxes, etc, and some ping pong balls, styrofoam packing chips, wrapped candies, or other similar small items. Each of you estimates how many of the items can be fit into each container. Fill each one absolutely full, write down the answers, and compare the results.

- When you pull into a parking lot with a reasonable number of cars, estimate how many cars there are. Now, drive slowly around the lot and count them.

- Get a measuring cup and different sizes of glasses. Fill the cup to an agreed upon level, such as ½ cup. Estimate which of the glasses will hold that much water, which will hold more, and which will overflow. Test your predictions.

- Once your child has familiarity with telling time, pick an activity like running around the house or doing jumping jacks. Estimate how many times you will be able to do it in 1 minute. Test your predictions. Try different activities and lengths of time.

- Do a combination physics and math activity. Make a ramp by raising up one end of a piece of wood with a support of some kind. You can also use a couple of sheets of cardboard taped together. Gather various round objects, like large and small balls, Styrofoam balls, baseball, basketball, etc. Work in an area with enough space in front of the ramp for the balls to roll down and stop on their own. Estimate how far each ball will roll and check your predictions.

Cooking

Your kitchen is a complete early learning center, with all kinds of practical life, sensory, math, science, and language activities. Food experiences are wonderful for teaching young children. Next are ideas for incorporating math into your daily food related activities.

Photo: Shutterstock

- Count everything. Pepperoni slices, utensils and plates, scoops of cereal, spoonfuls of ingredients – look for counting opportunities all the time. Whenever possible, line things up and count left to right to prepare for reading.

- Let your child measure out solid and liquid food items in a measuring cup. Even if she does not fully understand fractions, ounces, etc., this is all great experience: and these concepts can easily be taught using a simple measuring cup. Start by just showing your child the line to fill to, and the numeral next to it, such as ¼, ½, etc. As she gets more familiar, show her how 1 cup is divided into fractional parts.

- Plan recipes in advance and let your child help as he is able. If he is writing, he can write down items for the shopping trip. Take your child along to shop for the items and let her help find them and see their prices. Your child can then help make the recipe in every way he is able, such as counting out and measuring ingredients, mixing, spooning, etc.

- Work on fractions, as shown on p. 84-86. Have your child estimate where to cut to make two, three, and four equal size pieces of banana, celery, etc.

- Get your child an egg timer and let him set cooking and other time periods with it, such as how long to let a pie sit before it is cut. Once your child has learned a bit about telling time, have her watch the clock to know when something has cooked enough. Let your child enter cooking times on the microwave.

- Do operations with numbers. Four people who each eat 3 cookies means we need how many cookies (4X3)? Should we bake a few extra? If we put two eyes on each cookie face, how many eyes will we need? How many grapes from a bunch can each of three people have (divide the grapes from a bunch into 3 bowls)? How many 2" square brownies can we cut from the pan? Use a tape measure or ruler and mark off the 2" measurements with little notches in the large brownie, the cut between notches. Do simple addition and subtraction work whenever the opportunity presents itself.

- Teach your child simple proportions. If 1 egg is added to 2 cups of flour to make 12 of something, how many eggs and cups of flour will you need to make 24 or 36?

- Use a simple refrigerator thermometer and check the temperatures in the frig and freezer. Talk about how water freezes at 32 degrees F, and boils at 212 degrees F. Carefully boil water and use the thermometer to show this to your child, as well as teach safety around a hot stove, water, food, etc.

- Have everyone in your family rate meals on a 1-10 scale, where 1 means really didn't like this and 10 means loved it. Post results of many meals in your kitchen.

- Compare weights of different fruits and vegetables on a simple scale. If your child just cut a banana in two equal size pieces, do they weight the same?

Testing the Odds

A couple of simple activities will introduce your 5-6 year old child to the concept of probability:

- Show your child a quarter, and identify the heads and tails sides. Ask your child, *"If we flipped this coin and let it fall a bunch of times, can we guess which side will be up?"* Flip the coin 20 times and write down the results, heads or tails. Did one side appear more than the other? Why? Flip the coin another 10 times and recheck. As you do more flips, the numbers for each side should get closer. Repeat the activity, but this time have your child guess before each flip. Record how many times your child guessed right and how many wrong. How do these results compare with those in your first experiment?

- Get 9 M&M's in one color, and 1 in a different color. Put them all in a bag. Ask your child how many tries she thinks it will take before she pulls out the 1 M&M of a different color. Test it out a few times and write down how many times it took each time. What is the smallest number of tries and what is the largest? Next, try 2 of one color and 8 of another, then 3 & 7, 4 & 6, and 5 & 5. Write down the results as before. It should take less tries as the numbers get more equal. Why is that?

You can find fun probability activities to do on your computer at:

jmathpage.com/JIMSProbabilitypage.html

Conservation of Quantity

The Swiss developmental psychologist Jean Piaget once said, *"Only education is capable of saving our societies from possible collapse, whether violent or gradual."* Hard to argue with that. One observation Piaget made was that until children develop some abstract thinking ability, they do not understand that quantity remains the same even though displayed in different ways. Try these experiments out with your child. Most children begin to understand these concepts at around 5-7 years.

Gather a few differently shaped clear glass containers. One should be tall and narrow, another wide and short, and at least one more somewhere in between.

Get a measuring cup and have your child fill it up to the 1 cup line. Color the water with a little food coloring. Have him pour the fluid into one of the containers. Now repeat the process with the other two containers. If 1 cup is too little, use more. Line them up, and ask your child if one container has more than another, or if they all have the same.

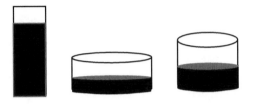

Most 3-5 year olds, even though they filled the measuring cup with 1 cup of water for each container, will say that the tall, narrow container has more water in it. When your child understands that they all have the same amount of water, you will know that she has developed some ability to use abstract thought.

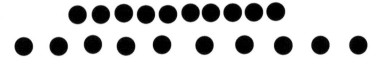

You can do a similar activity with coins. Have your child count out two rows of coins with the same number of coins in them, like 10. Now, spread the coins out in one row to make it longer, and ask your child if one row now has more than the other row. When your child knows that they still have the same number of coins, or realizes that it is necessary to count the coins to be certain, you will know that your child is becoming more able to use reasoning and abstract thought, a significant developmental task of the years 3-6.

"Children are human beings to whom respect is due, superior to us by reason of their innocence and of the greater possibilities of their future."

"Never help a child with a task at which he feels he can succeed."

Maria Montessori

A Parting Note

The activities in this book represent about how far a dedicated parent will take a 3-7 year old into math at home. Doing even the basic activities here regularly will give a child a great preparation for early success in math at school. If your child really gets into it, don't hesitate to take your home math farther into the decimal system, carrying numbers in subtraction and division, angles, and even simple equations. Memorizing the multiplication tables is practically a lost art, but gives a child a big advantage over depending on a calculator.

Our children today need a solid foundation in STEM – science, technology, engineering, and mathematics – studies to be prepared for the world they will experience throughout their lifetimes. Starting a child early is the best way to insure a comfort level and expectation of success with these subjects. There is an extensive science activities section in the Montessori At Home! eBook, and more activity descriptions online. Check them out and see where your child's interests lie. You just may ignite a flame of curiosity that will grow into a career.

Made in the USA
Middletown, DE
26 February 2017